TOWARD THE INTEGRATION
OF PSYCHOTHERAPY

WILEY SERIES ON PSYCHOLOGICAL DISORDERS

IRVING B. WEINER, Editor
School of Medicine and Dentistry
The University of Rochester

TOWARD THE
INTEGRATION OF
PSYCHOTHERAPY

JOHN M. REISMAN

Professor and Director of The Psychology Clinic
Memphis State University

Wiley-Interscience

A DIVISION OF JOHN WILEY & SONS, INC.

NEW YORK · LONDON · SYDNEY · TORONTO

Library of Congress Catalogue Card Number: 77-147236

ISBN 0-471-71570-0

Printed in the United States of America.

10 9 8 7 6 5 4 3 2 1

To Celia and Howard Jacobson

Series Preface

This series of books is addressed to behavioral scientists concerned with understanding and ameliorating psychological disorders. Its scope should prove pertinent to clinicians and their students in psychology, psychiatry, social work, and other disciplines that deal with problems of human behavior as well as to theoreticians and researchers studying these problems. Although many facets of behavioral science have relevance to psychological disorder, the series concentrates on the three core clinical areas of psychopathology, personality assessment, and psychotherapy.

Each of these clinical areas can be discussed in terms of theoretical foundations that identify directions for further development, empirical data that summarize current knowledge, and practical applications that guide the clinician in his work with patients. The books in this series present scholarly integrations of such theoretical, empirical, and practical approaches to clinical concerns. Some pursue the implications of research findings for the validity of alternative theoretical frameworks or for the utility of various modes of clinical practice; others consider the implication of certain conceptual models for lines of research or for the elaboration of clinical methods; and others encompass a wide range of theoretical, research, and practical issues as they pertain to a specific psychological disturbance, assessment technique, or treatment modality.

IRVING B. WEINER

University of Rochester
Rochester, New York

Preface

In his book *Comparative Psychology of Mental Development* Heinz Werner described a major hypothesis concerning the direction of growth. He stated that there is progress from a condition of relative undifferentiation toward a greater articulation of parts. Moreover, he noted that this process of differentiation must be balanced by a process of integration. If it were not, the development would be fragmented.

The field of psychotherapy certainly gives evidence of differentiation. Everywhere there are variety and innovation. New techniques, new organizations, new journals, new ways of looking at things are reported almost daily. They attest to the vigor and creative energy of psychotherapists, but they are not all that is needed for optimum growth. Integration is also needed.

This book provides a step in the process of integrating psychotherapy by identifying it. In so doing it not only points out commonalities among diverse systems and practices within psychotherapy, but also affords access for the integration of psychotherapy with other areas of knowledge. It is addressed to all who are interested in psychotherapy as it has been defined, and to all who may become interested in it as it is defined in these pages.

An assumption in the writing of this book is that psychotherapy, as a rough approximation to its identity, is something that a psychotherapist does. It is an activity, which must be specified independently of its presumed consequences. The effects or success of psychotherapy, although of great practical importance, are irrelevant to its definition.

Our attention is thus directed to the activities of the therapist, rather than to the responses of the client. This focus has the salutary effect of reducing the mystique that often is introduced into discussions of psychotherapy and has the additional benefit of placing the theoretical systems into a somewhat different perspective than is customary. Within this context they are viewed as significant only to the extent that they influence practice and are communicated to clients.

Chapter 1 presents an evaluation of a representative selection of definitions of psychotherapy. There are, of course, more definitions that could have been mentioned, but the purpose of this chapter was not to present an exhaustive list, merely an illustrative one. Nevertheless, it is sufficiently thorough to enable a reasonable impression to be gained of the different meanings offered for psychotherapy, of the issues that these different meanings represent, and of the categories into which definitions other than those considered might be ordered.

The chapters that follow explore the ways in which the meeting, the time, the therapist, and the process of communication have been varied and manipulated. Here the purpose is to consider the dimensions along which psychotherapists differ in their practices in order to arrive at a precise, recognizable definition of psychotherapy. The emphasis is on the extremes, the limits of variation, so as to note what is and what is not essential to the definition.

The final two chapters discuss some of the pertinent assumptions that therapists have about man and his behavior and trace the implications of the definition that emerges from this book. Research possibilities are outlined, some of my own work in this area is described, and the relevance of the definition for professionals and for the public is made clear.

I thank Irving Weiner and Gardner Spungin for their constructive suggestions and criticisms. Thanks are also due Werner Halpern, Robert Vidulich, Micky Kirk, Bill Tuberville, John Johnson, and my wife, Margo, who provided help and encouragement along the way.

Grateful acknowledgment is also given to Lyle Stuart for permission to use the quotations which appear as chapter epigraphs in this book. They are to be found in *The Great Quotations,* compiled by George Seldes, published in a Pocket Book edition by Simon and Schuster. Similarly, I am grateful to *Mental Hygiene* for permission to make use of the material which constitutes much of Chapter 1; this will appear in a somewhat modified version as an article in that journal. Finally, I thank Ada Marie Bell for her aid in typing the references.

JOHN M. REISMAN

October 1970
Memphis, Tennessee

Contents

TOWARD THE INTEGRATION
OF PSYCHOTHERAPY

INTRODUCTION

The Troubles Besetting Psychotherapy and a Proposed Solution

We have heard it said that there is not a Quaker or a Baptist, a Presbyterian or an Episcopalian, a Catholic or a Protestant in heaven; that on entering the gate, we leave those badges of schism behind. . . . Let us not be uneasy than about the different roads we may pursue, as believing them the shortest, to that our last abode.

Thomas Jefferson

It is difficult to believe that at the beginning of the twentieth century there was no professional practice of psychotherapy because today signs of its importance are evident everywhere. Professional organizations and journals in psychiatry, psychology, and social work attest to the permanence and vigor of psychotherapy, with each year bringing additional hundreds of publications to describe its practice, report its research, and detail its successes. This interest is not confined to the scientific community, but is widely shared by the educated public. Newspaper articles, television, motion pictures, and popular books and magazines have given considerable attention to psychotherapy, almost always reflecting positive, favorable attitudes. They have presented deeply moving case studies of treatment, unsolicited, hence all the more impressive, endorsements by celebrities who themselves have experienced its benefits, and enthusiastic reports of its many innovations. Understandably, the public views psychotherapy as a treatment method that is highly demanding, enormously desirable, and justly in need of support through federal, state, and local funds. Yet there is a great discrepancy between the public's evaluation of psychotherapy and that of many professionals.

Psychotherapists see a situation in which their craft, despite its public success and acceptance, has been subjected to criticism and derogation by their professional colleagues. They are very much aware of the different forms of psychotherapy, which at times are presented as competitive, rather

1

than as complementary. They have witnessed arguments that have challenged the efficacy of one or another of their procedures, and they have been exposed to legal battles that have challenged the qualifications of one or another professional group of practitioners. They have been urged to undergo lengthy and intensive training before judging themselves competent to engage in practice, and they are obliged to continue to refine their skills throughout their careers; yet they are also told that these acquired skills are of relatively little importance in being therapeutic. For approximately twenty years they have read and heard debates about the value and significance of psychotherapy, and this ceaseless questioning is widely held to be inconclusive so that a persistent doubt has been raised about the worth of this method.

This doubt, often not openly expressed, has had a major effect on the course of psychotherapy during the 1960s. One result has been the call by some therapists for the creation of their field as a profession in its own right, with the formation of special schools and institutes dedicated exclusively to the training of students as psychotherapists. The argument in favor of teaching psychotherapy as a special skill has emphasized both its rigorous nature and the importance of its being taught in an atmosphere of congeniality, the implication being that students can neither learn nor practice this method properly when they are instructed by those who have little faith in its usefulness, and that this is all too often the case in existing schools. Psychotherapy, it is argued, *is* an effective method of treatment when the therapist can convey to his clients confidence in the value of what they are doing.

A second result is a growing belief in the therapist's personality as crucial in determining the success of treatment. This belief is based on a mounting body of evidence that indicates that it is no longer sufficient to be schooled thoroughly in theory and technique. There must, these studies suggest, be certain warm human qualities that can be shared in the relationship, and the sharing of these qualities is necessary to bring about constructive changes in the client's attitudes and behavior. Further, it is alleged that therapists who are detached, aloof, and unresponsive to their clients' feelings may not only fail to help, but actually worsen their clients' conditions.

These findings are deceptive in their simplicity for they have unsettling implications. Although students of psychotherapy are screened for desirable personality characteristics, much of the research in this area has been conducted with professional therapists. Accordingly, a discontinuity has been introduced between professional training and effectiveness. The fact that a therapist may have excellent credentials is apparently no assurance that he can be of benefit to his clients. Rather it is the nature of his personality functioning that may make him an appropriate or inappropriate agent of treatment. Quite sensibly it has been proposed that these favorable characteristics should be sought in the selection of mental health professionals and developed in their training.

However, there remains the matter of evaluating the personalities of therapists who are already in practice to determine if they are best advised to limit themselves to a certain clientele or to abandon their treatment efforts entirely. This proposal is reasonable and in the interests of both the public and the professions concerned. For the contention has been made on the basis of sound research that psychotherapy *is* an effective method of treatment whose successes have been obscured by the failures of therapists whose personalities have been detrimental to the welfare of their clients.

A third important result has derived a vigorous impact from its confluence with other seemingly unrelated forces: the booming population; the unrelenting and increasing pressures for social reform and the eradication of poverty conditions; and the limited ability of schools, clinics, hospitals, and professionals to respond to the needs for their services.

Early in the 1960s Leon Eisenberg (1961) took note of the alarming fact that only 250 certified child psychiatrists existed in the United States while conservative estimates placed the number of emotionally disturbed school-age children at about two million. Equally distressing manpower shortages were noted in clinical psychology and social work.

Clearly the personnel at hand could not be expected to deal with the problem of mental illness by continuing to offer treatment largely through forms of individual psychotherapy. Such efforts were not only inordinately time-consuming, but also were reported to have been inappropriate in dealing with the psychological problems of the poor. Therefore it was questioned whether it was wise even to attempt to meet the need through the expansion of training programs that would only turn out professionals schooled in the customary procedures. New approaches were needed, principally ones that would be concerned with the prevention of disturbances, as well as with their alleviation.

The rationale for prevention is straightforward and compelling. It has been amply documented that a deplorable environment produces people who are bitter, frustrated, and without hope. Men, women, and children who suffer material and psychological deprivations can reasonably be expected to be unhappy. In particular, the conditions of poverty under which many Americans live, frequently aggravated by prejudice and the denial of opportunities, are virtually certain to yield feelings of depression and rage. Here is the kind of social situation where a change for the better could have favorable psychological consequences for a vast number of individuals. By becoming involved in changes in society, rather than concentrating their energies only on the problems of specific clients, psychiatrists, psychologists, and social workers might help to bring about a community that would ameliorate existing disorders and prevent the occurrence of others. This would be a way of dealing with mental illness on a grand scale, and it would enable a limited number of skilled personnel to have a beneficial effect on large populations.

But the treatment of persons already disturbed and those who would become disturbed still had to be provided. How were they to be helped at a time when the demands upon professional activities were growing? Efficient uses of limited professional time seemed to be the answer, and no suggestion appeared to be more promising for promoting efficiency than having therapists help other people to perform as therapists, or in a therapeutic manner.

Thus there arose an unprecedented interest in allowing and encouraging nonprofessionals to assume therapeutic roles. Housewives, volunteers, neighbors, parents, friends were enlisted as agents in supplying psychological assistance, usually under the guidance and with the support of professional consultants. Initially regarded as an expedient, as a means to provide some help to persons who otherwise would have received none, the employment of nonprofessionals came to be viewed increasingly as the best method to aid certain population groupings. The favorable response to these innovations also suggested an explanation for the difficulties that therapists had experienced in attempting to work with lower-class clients. The fault, it now appeared, was neither with the method of treatment offered, psychotherapy, nor with the clientele, but with the person who was trying to offer assistance. Through no fault of his own the therapist was unable to understand or to be understood by those who differed from him in several crucial respects. In other words, this argument went, psychotherapy *is* an effective method of treatment when the therapist has those characteristics that allow him to be accepted by his client, and those therapists who differ from their clients in race, socioeconomic status, and culture are handicapped in being able to serve them.

A fourth result of the doubt about the effectiveness of psychotherapy has been the growing acceptance of the premise that psychotherapy is ineffective. The advocates of this position contend that this has been amply demonstrated by the failures of studies to find significant differences between treated and untreated groups. The passage of time alone, they suggest, is the major identifiable variable which can account for improvement. Although it is to be regretted, it must be concluded that psychotherapy as it has been practiced and its attendant theories are just so many blind alleys.

What is needed, the argument proceeds, is a break with the tradition of the past thirty or forty years and a return to the points of view that were abandoned prematurely during the early part of the twentieth century. When we look at things "fresh," we can see that much that we thought of as products of unconscious conflicts or as symptoms of mental illnesses can be considered profitably as simply acquired patterns of behavior. These bits of behavior, these habits, fears, and acts, were learned. Moreover, they are being maintained by rewards that the individual receives for their performance. It follows, therefore, that they can be extinguished, and that new, appropriate behaviors can be taught through the judicious use of the principles of learning.

Thus far these learning principles have been disarmingly simple. If we wish a response to be repeated, we reward its occurrence (reinforcement). If we wish a response to occur, we reward responses that approximate it, gradually demanding that they more closely approximate the desired behavior in order to be rewarded (shaping responses). If we wish to extinguish a response, we do not reward its occurrence (nonreinforcement), punish its occurrence (avoidant conditioning), or elicit mutually exclusive responses to the same stimuli (enable the person to feel relaxed in a situation where he formerly felt anxious, as in reciprocal inhibition). It is preferable to reward behavior that is desirable than to punish behavior that is undesirable, since the latter strategy does not specify the action to be followed.

Further, the advocates of this position have frequently asserted, though it is not essential to their stand for them to have done so, that unconscious conflicts, if such do exist, need not concern us. Moreover, in great contrast to their colleagues, they have minimized the significance of the quality of the relationship with the client, so long as it is a cooperative one.

They have presented their case straightforwardly. The therapist is an expert in the modification of human behavior, and his job is to tell the person what to do, or to get him to do what should be done, so that symptoms are alleviated and desirable responses are developed. Traditional psychotherapy is an unsystematic application of learning principles, and it could benefit greatly if its therapists made use of these principles deliberately. In the meantime, behavior therapy is a planned, almost irresistible attack that can achieve some success with the most difficult of cases and with great economy.

Each of the last three results or developments is predicated upon the acknowledged deficiencies of psychotherapy as it has been, and still largely is, practiced. The second and third developments are compatible; they urge the helping person to make contact with another human being in a deep, intimately friendly way in order to be of service to him. One urges the therapist to greater personal involvement and to an uncompromisingly warm feeling toward one's fellow man, but is silent on what is to be done if the therapist cannot marshal warmth during the treatment hour. The other explicitly cautions therapists to recognize their limitations in being able to establish meaningful relationships; and it advises that therapeutic gains can be achieved by our assistance to those who are not mental health professionals but who can quite readily establish, or who are already involved in, such relationships with persons in need of help. The fourth result is the most radical departure for it assumes that therapeutic failures cannot be remedied by somehow changing the intensity of the relationship, but only by drastic changes in treatment philosophy and technique.

The majority of therapists have been trained in treatment approaches where an emphasis on the significance of their relationship with their clients is congenial with their own beliefs and values. Most of them do not feel personally threatened by any requirement that they transmit greater sensitivity and warmth. However, they are less comfortable with assertions that, regardless of their dedication and skill, there are clients whom they cannot reach and help through no fault of their own, but because of differences in race and culture. In this same vein they are also troubled by demands that they leave their offices and go into the community in the role of a consultant, a task for which some feel neither prepared nor inclined. Furthermore, they experience a growing apprehension that in their zeal to serve the public they may make sacrifices greater than those they intended, a sentiment Arnhoff (1968) expressed in this manner: "Psychology exclusively owns precious little today compared to a few years ago. It increasingly shares its prized service activities with many other groups, many of whom are trained in a shorter period of time and who come cheaper in the marketplace."

Nor do some therapists hasten to embrace suggestions that they make greater use of learning techniques and play a more authoritative, tutorial role with their clients. Both by training and inclination they simply do not feel able to perform in this manner. Furthermore, they are skeptical about the studies that have investigated the applications of learning principles, distressed about the possible depersonalization of clients, and uneasy that these methods at times appear to achieve their successes by a sacrifice of sensitivity and a touch of ruthlessness. Yet despite their misgivings they see graduate schools teaching behavior modification to students, and discussions of this treatment occupying an ever more prominent place in professional journals and meetings.

Thus a set of circumstances exists that is divisive and disheartening to many professional psychotherapists who would like to feel themselves banded together with their colleagues and working cooperatively. Instead, within recent years separate organizations of psychotherapists have formed, which differ not only in theory and technique as previous organizations, but which also see themselves differing in their fundamental values and attitudes about man. Meanwhile, there is no shortage of critics outside the field of psychotherapy to discount the worth of this method of treatment, and no end to the advisors and standard-bearers within it to urge therapists to abandon what they are doing and to try some new approach or technique.

It no longer is enough to say of this state of affairs that it is "exciting" and "challenging." These are excitements and challenges born of discontinuities, and as such they tend to arouse uncertainties about identity and to foster a condition that promotes fragmentation of the field. Although differentiation as a process is one aspect of healthy growth, it needs to be balanced properly by synthetization if an excessive fragmentation and a loss of identity are to be avoided.

Synthetization as a process can be advanced in two major ways. One way would be to call upon higher levels of abstraction which would perforce embrace all psychotherapists. For example, therapists would be reminded that they share a common globe with its universal problems and needs for brotherhood, peace, and a good life. The difficulty with this approach is that since the attributes are not distinctive to psychotherapists, the basic question of professional identity would not have been answered. Instead, it would be sidestepped, and the bonds of integration among therapists as therapists would be no stronger than before.

The second way would be to direct attention to the many differences in the conduct of psychotherapy, to seek out the structure that courses through its variety of forms, and to discover what provides a framework for its systems. This analysis would be an identification of what is integrative in psychotherapy, and therefore it would set boundaries to the field. It is the plan that will be followed in this book.

The procedure that will be employed will accomplish the following. First, a wide variety of ways of doing psychotherapy will be set down so that the range of what has been done is made known. Second, ideas of the dimensions along which psychotherapy has been varied will be gained, and this will enable modifications of psychotherapy to be ordered that have not been considered specifically and that may be proposed in the future. Third, some possible variations of therapy that seem to be indicated will be suggested. Fourth, areas of research will be pointed out. Fifth, psychotherapy will be defined, and its terms and implications will be made clear.

It is the issue of the definition of psychotherapy which is at the core of this analysis. Incredible as it may seem, there is no scientifically serviceable definition of psychotherapy. Small wonder, then, that the boundaries of psychotherapy seem diffuse, and it is alleged, without any means for substantiation or refutation, that this group or that group is engaged in its practice. At the heart of the problem is confusion about what psychotherapy is.

Accordingly, in Chapter 1 a representative sample of definitions of psychotherapy will be evaluated. At the outset it should be made clear that some of these definitions have attempted to describe psychotherapy as a special kind of beneficial or learning process. Such a conceptualization immediately introduces a serious error and source of disorder. It equates the method with its presumed consequences so that identification of it is contingent on the existence of certain effects. It narrows understanding by precluding the possibility that psychotherapy can be practiced without any notable success.

There is no justification for believing that psychotherapy is invariably psychotherapeutic, just as it is incorrect to assume that because improvements in behavior and psychological well-being are observed then psychotherapy has been practiced. To examine this subject without bias, the position will be adopted that, put broadly, psychotherapy is what the person who practices this method of treatment does. The effects and the effectiveness of what he does will be regarded as other issues that are irrelevant to the purpose at hand; although, in the end, these are the issues that are of the greatest importance to society and to therapists.

It has been claimed that while therapists differ considerably in their theories, the differences between them in actual practice are less striking. From Chapter 2 on, this contention will be tested by an examination of what therapists do and the manipulations that can be made in the treatment interview. The strategy here is to regard the various theories as systems of understanding and to attend not so much to these systems as to the means by which they are implemented. This should make for a more parsimonious approach than a consideration of theories, since if therapists do the same thing, it makes little difference to clients or observers that they do so for a number of different reasons.

The goal of this appraisal of a diversity of explicit methods and techniques is to find what integrates and unifies psychotherapy and to extract a definition that makes clear strategies for research and that promotes understanding. In Chapter 6, the implications of this definition for the professional conduct of psychotherapy and for interpersonal relationships in general will be discussed. These implications suggest that psychotherapy should not be viewed as a process confined to the therapist's office, but that it be conceived of as a communication, and hence capable of being expressed in virtually all human interactions.

CHAPTER 1

Toward the Definition of Psychotherapy

The aim of science is to seek the simplest explanation of complex facts. We are apt to fall into the error of thinking that the facts are simple because simplicity is the goal of our quest. The guiding motto in the life of every natural philosopher should be, "Seek Simplicity and distrust it."

Alfred North Whitehead

Science is simply common sense at its best—that is, rigidly accurate in observation, and merciless to fallacy in logic.

Thomas H. Huxley

A reasonable first step in the evaluation of any subject is to define it. By defining the subject, a means is provided for setting limits, for making clear what something is and what it is not. There is little controversy about the desirability of that objective, though its feasibility is often disputed on the grounds that to do so would be premature since there is insufficient knowledge about the subject. Such a misgiving has been expressed in relation to psychotherapy, but it is preferable to have a definition that approximates the "truth" than to have nothing at all.

Moreover, psychotherapists have not been remiss in attempting to meet their responsibility to define psychotherapy. As might be expected, however, in a field such as this one where so much has been written from so many points of view, various types of definitions have been offered. The task of this chapter is to assess each of these types and to make explicit in what ways they may have failed to clarify their subject. In order to do so, a number of definitions will be presented to illustrate how psychotherapy has been defined, and to communicate the feelings and ideas that therapists have sought to convey about their field.

Some of these definitions are very different from others, not only in denotation, but intent. To be sure, some were not intended to serve a scientific purpose, and their authors are fully aware of the limitations their definitions have when they are judged in that sense, some were offered

9

casually, and some were offered after much reflection and thought. Yet all have found their way into print, from where they may serve to inform or to perplex the professional community and the public. Unquestionably, some of these definitions are better than others, and surely each has its critics as well as its supporters. How can it be decided which among them has merit for an integrative approach to psychotherapy? In other words, what are the characteristics of a "good," "scientifically satisfactory" definition?

STANDARDS FOR DEFINING PSYCHOTHERAPY

One standard that can be used has been proposed by lexicographers. They advise that a definition should not be arbitrary, which is to say that a proposed meaning should not depart radically from previous concepts about the word. This is immediately helpful because "psychotherapy" is not an esoteric term, and therefore a crude approximation to its meaning can quickly be reached. Since the public already knows that in a broad sense psychotherapy refers to the alleviation or treatment of psychological disturbances, it is preferable to have a definition that at least retains the spirit of that meaning. Conversely, it would be undesirable to accept what is an idiosyncratic use of the word.

Second, all things being equal, it would also seem prudent to favor definitions that are precise, that state in a fairly specific and concrete way what psychotherapy is. Such definitions would enable someone to distinguish between what is psychotherapeutic, which conceivably could be almost anything, and what is psychotherapy, which refers to a particular method of treatment. It would be ideal to find a definition that identifies psychotherapy and its operations without depending on the appraisals or stated intentions of someone else, a definition that strikes a correct balance between being inclusive of all that legitimately falls within that field and being exclusive of all that does not properly belong there. In short, a definition that tells the essential characteristics of psychotherapy so that others can recognize it in all its ordinarily accepted forms.

Finally, it is better to define psychotherapy as it is, rather than according to what it is intended to do. Among the aims of psychotherapy are the provision of a relationship, the promotion of a process, and the stimulation of emotional experiences. But when psychotherapy is defined by these goals or hoped-for effects, it follows by the definition that the method cannot be said to exist unless those effects exist. For example, if psychotherapy is defined as a certain kind of process or relationship and the therapist reports that after a number of meetings that relationship or process did not occur, then it would follow that those meetings did not contain psychotherapy.

Some therapists would say that these were "pre-therapy sessions." Such definitions make it impossible to acknowledge that the method has any failings, and they create uncertainty about what is occurring during that time when the objectives have yet to be reached. These are serious and apparently unnecessary limitations. Accordingly, definitions that emphasize the responses of the client will be rejected, and the standard will be adopted that the meaning be confined to an explicit statement based upon the performance of the therapist.

These three standards, recognizability, precision, and independence from goals, will be the guides in evaluating the definitions that follow.

PSYCHOTHERAPY DEFINED BY ITS GOALS

There are 31 definitions that have been selected to illustrate the four major ways in which psychotherapy has been defined. The first group defines psychotherapy according to its goals, that is, psychotherapy is whatever is used to attain a certain objective or whatever serves a particular purpose. Therefore, these definitions clearly violate the standard of independence from goals, and thus they are unacceptable. Nevertheless, they are instructive because they make clear with simplicity, at times with elegance, some of the aims of psychotherapists.

1. "The art of treating mental diseases or disorders. Any measure, mental or physical, that favorably influences the mind or psyche" (Hinsie and Shatsky, 1947).

2. ". . . the use of measures which it is believed will act upon the patient's mind and thereby promote his mental health and aid his adjustment to the particular problems which have disturbed his happiness or adaptation" (Noyes, 1948).

3. ". . . a method of treatment which aims to help the impaired individual by influencing his emotional processes, his evaluation of himself and of others, his evaluation of and his manner of coping with the problems of life" (Maslow and Mittelman, 1951).

4. ". . . the science or art of curing psychological abnormalities and disorders" (Barnhart, 1951).

5. ". . . the art and science of treating mental and emotional disorders and diseases through changing ideas and emotions to bring about a more favorable psychic equilibrium" (English and Finch, 1954).

These definitions are singularly uninformative about the methods or measures used in psychotherapy, and in some instances this has been by intention. The aim, perhaps, has been to be inclusive, but the result is a failure to specify what is distinctive about this form of treatment. Were someone seriously to adopt this kind of definition, he would find it impossible to tell when psychotherapy was being practiced by an independent observation. The only available standard would be the intent or purpose ascribed to his actions by the "therapist." While there is nothing intrinsically wrong in trusting the judgment of the practitioner to know when he is trying to conduct psychotherapy, it would be better, both for him and for others who wish to build a science, to have a means of appraisal that does not rely upon his intentions.

Moreover, each definition implies, and that of Hinsie and Shatsky specifically states, that any measure may be regarded as part of psychotherapy if it has some beneficial effect upon a person's mental health. This blurs the distinction between what is psychotherapeutic and what is psychotherapy and leads to a concept of the term that does not correspond to its popular meaning. People do not think of brain surgery, drugs, entertainments, electroshocks, or pleasant dinners as forms of psychotherapy. Nor do they believe the spankings and assorted punishments of their childhood were instances of this type of treatment, even when they are willing to concede that they were genuine parental attempts to remedy certain psychological abnormalities. Instead, it is generally recognized that talk of a highly personal nature is involved in psychotherapy; therefore, mention of such communication should be found in a definition that is satisfactory. Definitions which lack even this small degree of specificity err seriously in the direction of vagueness and overinclusiveness.

PSYCHOTHERAPY DEFINED BY ITS TYPE OF PROCEDURES

The definitions in this group state in a broad way the measures that are employed in the practice of psychotherapy. To that extent they unify the field, and have the added advantage of not only agreeing with the popular concept, but also of expressing a degree of sophistication sufficient to satisfy many professionals.

1. ". . . the utilization of psychological measures in the treatment of sick people" (Romano, 1947).

2. ". . . the employment of mental factors in the treatment of disease" (Rosanoff, 1947).

3. ". . . the art of combatting disease and promoting health by mental influences" (Whitehorn, 1948).

4. ". . . a multitude of psychological methods all having one thing in

common—the intent to help a suffering individual through psychological means" (Grotjohn and Gabe, 1950).

5. ". . . the treatment of mental or physical disorder by using mental influences" (Yates, 1951).

6. "Mental treatment of illness, especially of nervous diseases and maladjustments, as by suggestion, psychoanalysis, or re-education" (Neilson, 1952).

7. ". . . the method which tries to achieve this goal (eliminating or rendering harmless the seat of a disease) by psychologic means" (Deutsch and Murphy, 1960).

8. "The treatment of mental illness and mild adjustment problems by means of psychological techniques" (Morgan, 1961).

9. "Certain types of therapy rely primarily on the healer's ability to mobilize healing forces in the sufferer by psychological means. These forms of treatment may be generically termed psychotherapy" (Frank, 1961, p. 1).

10. "Psychotherapy . . . means the use of verbal methods in interpersonal relationships with the intent of assisting a person or persons to modify attitudes and behavior which are intellectually, socially or emotionally maladaptive" (University of the State of New York, 1961).

Although these definitions are both specific and inclusive—for example, Frank did wish to include the work done by religious healers and shamans—they lack the specificity to exclude techniques and procedures that do not properly belong to psychotherapy, for example, "brainwashing," taunting, ridicule, sarcasm, public relations, advertising, and propaganda. These are psychological measures that are neither thought of as psychotherapy nor ordinarily used in treating emotional disorders. Therefore, the definitions of this group are not sufficiently precise to enable discriminations between psychological procedures that are employed in psychotherapy and those that are not. However, they suggest that a satisfactory definition would enable us to make such a discrimination.

The next group of definitions has succeeded in delineating the method with greater precision by introducing the qualifications of the practitioner as a limiting variable. The question to be considered is whether this restriction is valid.

PSYCHOTHERAPY DEFINED BY THE PRACTITIONER

As might be expected, professional interests play a role in how narrowly or broadly the qualifications of the practitioner are defined. Traditionally, members of the medical profession have been most careful to specify psychotherapy as a medical responsibility. The definition by Levine (1948) restricts psychotherapy to the physician—"psychotherapy means therapy by psychological means . . . (it) can be defined as the provision by the physician of new life experiences which can influence a patient in the direction of health"—while that of Polatin and Philtine (1949) more narrowly limits it to the psychiatrist: "a form of treatment in psychiatry in which the psychiatrist by his scientific thinking and understanding, attempts to change the thinking and feeling of people who are suffering from distorted mental or emotional processes." The American Psychiatric Association (1964) merely notes: "Most physicians regard intensive psychotherapy as a medical responsibility."

Other definitions, usually, but not always, advanced by members of nonmedical professions, are less restrictive.

1. ". . . the use of any psychological technique in the treatment of mental disorder or maladjustment . . . the term should be reserved for treatment by a professionally trained person—i.e., clinical psychologist, psychiatrist, or psychiatric social worker" (English and English, 1958).

2. ". . . any treatment in which the patient or client . . . talks to the doctor, therapist, or counselor during a series of sessions ranging in number from several to several hundred . . . mental or emotional disturbances are treated only through communication between patient and therapist" (Berelson and Steiner, 1964).

3. ". . . the use of learning or conditioning methods in a professional relationship to assist a person or persons to modify feelings, attitudes and behavior which are intellectually, socially or emotionally maladjustive or ineffectual" (American Psychological Association Committee on Legislation, 1967).

Although technically the next two definitions are more liberal, they are probably intended to be taken in the same spirit as the immediately preceding ones.

1. ". . . the treatment, by psychological means, of problems of an emotional nature in which a trained person deliberately establishes a professional relationship with the patient with the object (1) of removing, modifying, or retarding existing symptoms, (2) of mediating disturbed patterns of behavior, and (3) of promoting positive personality growth and development" (Wolberg, 1967, p. 3).

2. ". . . a prolonged interpersonal relationship between two or more people, one of whom has had special training in the handling of human relationships, using methods of a psychological nature" (Winder, 1957).

The last definition that we shall present in this group illustrates a type that is quite specific. It contends that a particular theory or way of doing psychotherapy is best, and then defines the method in such terms so as to exclude all therapies other than itself:

"True psychotherapy . . . can be effective only through the process of emotional regression and the reliving of traumatic feelings and memories of the past . . . . In this light, *psychotherapy can be defined as the process by which a patient is rendered accessible to the total educative influences of his world*" (Slavson, 1964).

These definitions may be evaluated from a legal and a scientific point of view. From the standpoint of law, it can readily be seen that they perform a highly important and necessary purpose. They serve to identify, more or less precisely, who may engage in the practice of psychotherapy, and thus they can provide some assurance that the public in purchasing this service will be protected from the incompetent and the unscrupulous. Legally, they can be considered sensible and useful.

However, from a scientific point of view these definitions leave much to be desired and are highly vulnerable in at least two areas. First, their specificity—they do not define psychotherapy itself with any greater precision than the definitions in the groups already considered, which, it will be recalled, were seriously deficient in that regard. Second, their validity—they restrict psychotherapy to those who are trained or members of a certain profession, and we must now ask if this limitation is logically or empirically valid. For this assertion to be valid logically, it would have to follow that the same behavior is not the same behavior when performed by different people. In order to be valid empirically, it would have to be demonstrated that only a given profession or professions are able to perform psychotherapy; when efforts are made by others to practice psychotherapy, their performance is not recognized to be an expression of this method of treatment.

Since it is not logical to argue that identical acts are different, it is clear that these definitions are not logically valid. However, since it is possible that acts that are supposed to be identical are in fact not identical, the matter of the empirical validity of these definitions would have to be settled. In turn, the question of their empirical validity can be determined through testing the following three assertions:

1. A specific method of psychotherapy is recognizably practiced only by the members of a given profession, for example, Rogerian therapy can be practiced well only by psychologists.

2. Only one specific system of psychotherapy has been found to be of value.

3. Psychotherapy is recognizably practiced only by those who have received a prescribed course of training.

Although these contentions have been long debated and have produced over the years an awesome volume of argument, the facts in relation to them, unfortunately, are modest and not particularly impressive. For example, the American Psychoanalytic Association, despite the emphatic disclaimers of Sigmund Freud himself, has had the policy that the practice of psychoanalysis or intensive, deep, reconstructive psychotherapy is the exclusive responsibility of the medical profession. While there is much that has been said in favor of this policy, there is no experimental evidence to justify it, and the number of competent and distinguished analysts and therapists who are not physicians would seem to refute the notion that medical training is essential to practice this treatment. A similar statement can be made for any specific system of psychotherapy; thus the first contention can be rejected because it can easily be demonstrated that virtually every one of these methods has eminent practitioners from at least two different professions.

The second assertion also has no evidence in its favor, and a great deal of evidence that could be brought to bear against it. Although it is probable that some systems of psychotherapy are more effective than others in certain cases, practically every system has reported that it is of value to some clients (Eysenck, 1961). Thus it would seem to be safe to reject this contention.

The third contention, however, still appears to be viable. While there is no experimental evidence to support it, there is as yet little data with which to refute it (Poser, 1966; Vesprani, 1969). It is possible that psychotherapy is recognizably practiced only by those who have received a definite course of training. What professionals would expect is that the trained person, in contrast to the untrained, would act more frequently, or consistently, in a manner that would be judged to be psychotherapy. Yet if this prediction is to be tested, there must be a definition of psychotherapy so as to enable judgments of its existence to be made.

Have we come full circle? Before a decision can be made about the relevance of training, there must be a definition of psychotherapy that can allow a grading of skill and effectiveness along that dimension. Such a definition has not been found in this group which has implied the importance of training.

Similarly, it is of little help in formulating a definition to abstract what is universal in all the forms of psychotherapy with the aim of uncovering what there is that is curative. To illustrate: Frank (1961, p. 62) has suggested that a common therapeutic agent is the arousal of the client's hope of recovery. This suggestion is perceptive and reasonable, and there is research to support it provided by studies by Friedman (1963) and Nash and Zimring (1969). The report by Friedman is especially interesting and pertinent.

Following their first treatment interview, 43 outpatients who had been diagnosed as neurotic were asked if they had experienced any relief of their symptoms. It was found that those patients who were quite hopeful about being helped reported a reduction in the intensity of their symptoms, particularly in their feelings of anxiety and depression. Friedman concluded that: "expectancy of help . . . may be an important determinant of symptom reduction in neurotic outpatients." Unfortunately, while this may point out what is therapeutic, it still does not specify what is psychotherapy, or what the therapist does in an effort to arouse the hope of the client, that is, to "mobilize healing forces." That is what is needed.

The same kind of criticism can be made of the definitions of a number of investigators who have been impressed by the relationship that ideally exists between the therapist and client. They have sought to define psychotherapy as this special kind of relationship, and their definitions and attempts to express what takes place shall next be considered.

PSYCHOTHERAPY DEFINED BY THE RELATIONSHIP

It is true that by reading these definitions some feeling for this method of treatment and for the diverse ways by which it is viewed and practiced can be gained. There are the matter-of-fact definitions:

1. "Psychotherapy is an exercise in cooperation and a test of cooperation. We can succeed only if we are genuinely interested in the other" (Adler, 1931).

2. ". . . a certain kind of social relationship between two persons who hold periodic conversations in pursuit of certain goals: namely, the lessening of emotional discomfort and the alteration of various other aspects of client behavior" (Shoben, 1953).

3. ". . . a learning process, and learning requires involvement with other people. That such cannot be replaced by drugs or by electrical or chemical procedures is quite obvious" (Ruesch, 1961).

4. ". . . a procedure wherein two persons engage in a prolonged series of emotion-arousing interactions, mediated primarily by verbal exchanges, the purpose of which is to produce changes in the behaviors of one of the pair" (Ford and Urban, 1963).

5. "Psychotherapy is viewed as a lawful influence process within the

broader context of studies of behavior control, studies which investigate the conditions that change behavior" (Krasner, 1963).

6. ". . . those methods which depend on a direct interaction between patient and therapist . . . . Its benefit lies in the relearning or new learning that the patient is able to accomplish through talk with the therapist and through the ensuing personal relation" (White, 1964).

And there are descriptions that convey that something essential about psychotherapy cannot be expressed by words alone:

1. "Therapy cannot do anything to anybody—hence can better represent a process going on, observed perhaps, understood perhaps, but not applied" (Taft, 1933).

2. "The therapeutic process occurs as a unique growth experience, created by one person seeking and needing help from another who accepts the responsibility of offering it" (Allen, 1942).

3. "It is a process, a thing-in-itself, an experience, a relationship, a dynamic. . . . Therapy is of the essence of life . . ." (Rogers, 1951).

4. ". . . therapy has to do with the *relationship,* and has relatively little to do with techniques or with theory and ideology" (Rogers, 1962).

5. "Especially inadequate is the term 'psychotherapy' to describe the kind of blossoming awareness and modification of interaction in all its complex varieties" (Blau, 1966).

No one who reads these definitions and statements can fail to be impressed by their earnestness and intensity. Nevertheless, it must also be recognized that not one of them actually tells what psychotherapy is. If two adults were observed seated in a room and engaged in conversation, it would be impossible to judge from these definitions whether psychotherapy was being practiced. Not only do they fail to define psychotherapy, but they inadvertently confuse the issue by confounding an intended effect with the procedure by means of which that effect is supposed to be produced. They do not tell what the therapist does. They tell the favorable response of the client to the work of the therapist.

Psychotherapy should be conceived of as a stimulus, not as a response. A "certain kind of social relationship" and a "unique growth experience" are hoped-for effects of the treatment, but they are not the treatment. Consider the invalid conclusions that would follow if they were. First, if psychotherapy invariably involved the specified relationship and process, it would be a form of treatment that would enjoy the unique and enviable distinction of being always to some extent successful. Yet it is known that most studies report that approximately one-third of the clients seen in psychotherapy do not improve (Eysenck, 1961). Second, since the relationship and the process come about over time, inevitably there would be a period in which the client is being seen for psychotherapy, but presumably is not receiving it. Third, in cases where the relationship or process did not develop, psychotherapy would not have been practiced. Fourth, therapists would not themselves know when they were practicing psychotherapy by what they were doing but would have to monitor the client for the existence of the relationship or process. Definitions with implications such as these should not be accepted. They preclude the possibility of limits or deficiencies in the method, and they force psychotherapists into the awkward position of not being certain of whether they are practicing their craft until they have achieved some measure of success.

CONCLUSIONS

The definitions of psychotherapy that have been examined have not identified this method of treatment in a way that is at once recognizable, precise, and independent of any of its goals or effects. Some appear to have confused psychotherapy with what is psychotherapeutic, while others, not entirely of a different genre, express the assumption that the method has been practiced only in cases where it has attained some favorable result. Moreover, some of these definitions, whether deliberately or not, are divisive, narrowly expressive of professional or theoretical interests that are baldly asserted without any evidence to justify their acceptance.

Yet these definitions are not entirely without merit. They do provide a broad basis for evaluating what different psychotherapies have in common. They have stated that, in general, this is a treatment method that makes use of psychological measures in being of assistance to persons who experience feelings of distress and unhappiness. By implication they suggest that, at least on the part of the therapist, there is communication and a wish to be of help to someone else. Further, they connote an attitude of respect toward the person in need of assistance. These are the elements that may prove of use in formulating a definition of psychotherapy.

CHAPTER 2

Manipulations in the Meeting of Therapist and Client

Life is short, art long, occasion sudden; to make experiments dangerous; judgment difficult. Neither is it sufficient that the physician do his office, unless the patient and his attendants do their duty, and that externals are likewise well ordered.

Hippocrates

Psychotherapy is a generic term, which is to say that it embraces a wide variety of methods rather than referring to one particular way of doing treatment. Ford and Urban (1963), who in their book, *Systems of Psychotherapy,* discuss ten major approaches—Freudian, ego-analytic, Dollard and Miller's, Adlerian, Rankian, Rogerian, Horney's, existential, Sullivanian, and behavioristic—certainly recognized that they did not exhaust the subject. In a similar book by Patterson (1966), *Theories of Counseling and Psychotherapy,* ten approaches, among others, are presented and evaluated that did not receive particular attention in Ford and Urban—Frankl's logotherapy, Grinker's transactional approach, Kelly's psychology of personal constructs, Rotter's social learning approach, Ellis' rational-emotive psychotherapy, Phillip's interference theory approach, Bordin's approach, Thorne's approach, and Williamson's approach.

Even taken together, the chapters of these authors could easily have been increased, and this despite the fact that their attention was devoted to relatively popular theoretical positions and not to the large, and apparently uncontrollable, number of variations and refinements. For a case could be made for the position that every practitioner has his own more or less idiosyncratic theory, differing from that of his colleagues and evolving as a function of his own hour-to-hour, day-to-day, year-to-year experiences.

The unifying thread that runs through each of these many theories is that they represent attempts to understand human behavior and to explain to some extent why people behave as they do. These attempts at understanding signify the importance of that attribute to psychotherapists and to psychotherapy, and such a characteristic would seem to be essential to a satisfactory definition.

It is also true that the diversity of theories, in and of itself, is impressive. Some therapists have been stimulated by the many ideas expressed and have found a number of them helpful at one time or another in their practice. They are able to accept the different points of view, and they have not found them irreconcilable. Yet others have been puzzled by the diversity and by the fact that few ideas have been supplanted. This has suggested that perhaps the diversity is illusory and that therapists, despite their many theories, share a common core of essential beliefs about what is truly important to psychotherapy.

At the very least this diversity, whether apparent or real, signals the great need for caution and precision in this area. In the study of this field care must be taken to specify the form of psychotherapy under consideration and to be mindful of the possible hazards and of the injustices that can be done when generalizations are made to the entire area from the results of research done with one of its small parts. Further, it must be decided just how much should be included and excluded as examples of practices or techniques in psychotherapy. What is involved in this decision is another one. Given the absence of a satisfactory definition of psychotherapy, shall it be implicitly defined in a manner that is narrow or broad?

Clearly, an extremely narrow view of psychotherapy has already been rejected. There is just no evidence to support one, while the results of study after study support the contention that there is some value in each of several approaches. Accordingly, the course that will be followed here will strive to be an impartial and straightforward one. The publication of theories and techniques in scientific journals and books is an indication that the author wishes to share his ideas and to offer them for serious consideration, and that the editors, his professional colleagues, judge them to have some merit. For the most part, then, what shall serve as a guide is what professionals are willing to recognize as instances of psychotherapy in their journals and books.

However, there must also be some basis for discrimination other than publication, if for no other reason than that occasionally an author wishes to edify his colleagues by satire. To a degree, assistance is provided by the broad definition of psychotherapy, psychological measures that are employed in order to help persons who experience unhappiness or distress. But what is meant by "psychological measures," and how broadly should that term be used?

For example, should behavior modification and the use of various conditioning procedures be considered as part of psychotherapy? Wolpe has argued that they should (Wolpe, 1963; Wolpe and Lazarus, 1966). He bases his contention on an argument that can be analyzed into four main points: (a) behavior modification and conditioning procedures are psychotherapeutic; (b) "traditional" approaches have been successful only when they have inadvertently made use of behavior modification techniques and addressed themselves to the altering of habits; (c) since psychotherapy is a convenient term that is well known to the public, it would be prejudicial to the acceptance of behavior modification if it had to be labeled as something unfamiliar; and (d) the behavior modifier respects and wishes to help his patient in the same way that most psychotherapists do, that is, there is a similar relationship in behavior modification and in psychotherapy.

The first point can be rejected quickly on the grounds expounded earlier that everything that is psychotherapeutic is not psychotherapy. The second point is an allegation, which is somewhat in conflict with the fourth point and which certainly would be of considerable interest if put to the test. However, for the present, and in the absence of data to allow for its evaluation, it is best held in abeyance. The third point borders on the venal and has no scientific merit. Finally, the fourth point notes that there are common elements in behavior modification and psychotherapy. This is probably true of a good many human relationships, but it, nevertheless, does not compel us to regard them as identical. Moreover, as was previously discussed, the work of the therapist, not the relationship, is definitive of psychotherapy.

In point of fact, why do Wolpe and others even feel that it needs to be argued whether behavior modification is, or is not, an instance of psychotherapy? Evidently they are responding to some distinction that is held to be crucial, and that distinction is that therapists not only have an understanding about the person, but also that they seek to communicate that understanding to the person. This seems to be the difference between whether behavior modification methods are thought of as instances of psychotherapy or as the application of training principles. In the former case, there is a communication of understanding. In the latter case, something is done to the client or for the client, but with no effort made to communicate understanding. This difference illuminates what shall be taken as the meaning of "psychological measures"—devices predicated upon the use of communication. As a rough means of discrimination it might even be said that: To the extent that communication is explicitly involved in the helping process, the probability is greater that the procedure is an instance of psychotherapy; and conversely, and with more certainty, when there is no communication discernible in the helping process, that procedure is not part of psychotherapy.

Thus techniques that rely fundamentally and explicitly on communication in order to assist the person are those that shall be considered to be psychotherapy. This first step toward a definition is intended to eliminate drugs, shock, surgery, baths, food, exercise, sleep, and so forth from being thought of as part of this field, even though all of these things can serve as vehicles of communication and can promote the functioning and happiness of people. This criterion would also eliminate procedures, such as conditioning and reinforcement, when they have been applied with no effort made to communicate explicitly to the client their purpose or to solicit his cooperation. For example, the conditioning of autistic children and the use of token economies in institutional settings would not in themselves be regarded as psychotherapy, but as training.

On the other hand, at this time it is difficult to see how psychotherapy would differ from counseling. These two terms have appeared side by side in book titles (Rogers, 1942; Patterson, 1966; Truax and Carkhuff, 1967), and the distinctions between them that some professionals have tried to make have not been particularly convincing. Part of the problem may be that some professionals have tried to incorporate everything that a psychotherapist does under the heading of psychotherapy, and everything that a counselor does under the heading of counseling.

Brammer and Shostrom (1960) have suggested that psychotherapy and counseling be regarded as falling along a therapeutic psychology continuum. They explain that the methods differ in the following respects. Psychotherapy extends over a long period of time and seeks to deal with the unconscious conflicts of persons who evidence severe personality disturbances; its goal is to alter personality functioning. In contrast, counseling is of relatively brief duration and seeks to help relatively normal individuals deal with current problems; its goal is to assist the person during some situational crisis. These differences in intention, in goals, in duration, and in clientele, even if they did exist in all cases, and they do not, are secondary characteristics. They are not definitive because they do not tell in what way the counselor and the psychotherapist differ in their behavior. To the extent that counselors and psychotherapists use communication in the same way, they are doing the same thing.

Perhaps it would be most helpful in understanding this assertion if at this point attention is directed to an examination of a typical form of this method of treatment.

The stereotype of psychotherapy is the analyst seated with notebook in hand at a distance behind the recumbent client's head. Talk issues from the client in a relatively unchecked stream. Occasionally, the analyst asks for clarification or makes a comment that deftly cuts away the superficial content of the speech and leaves exposed a meaning that is at once satisfying and profound. This is psychotherapy as it has been portrayed, both seriously and comically, in countless motion pictures, magazine articles, television productions, and works of fiction.

Yet what many therapists conceive of as psychotherapy is less artificial in its use of conversation and less dramatic in its seating arrangement. They picture the client and the therapist sitting facing each other. The talk is more of a give-and-take style than a monologue or lecture, but still it is quite different from a customary conversation. For one thing, the therapist does not respond to statements of opinion or belief with expressions of his own personal convictions. For another, if challenged to argument or debate, the therapist calls attention to the challenge but does not yield to it. In short, in a variety of ways the therapist places the interests of the client at the heart of their interview.

Very often the therapist extends his restraint on self-expression and interest to the decor of his office. Usually the room is quite spartan. Its furnishings are bland and modest, obviously constructed for strength, durability, and economy instead of aiming for an aesthetic appeal. There are no photographs on the desk or walls, nothing to indicate whether the therapist has children or is married, no clue as to his religion or politics, no sign of any hobby or nonprofessional interest. However, there may be framed documents, which attest to his professional qualifications and competence, and a display of books and journals, which suggest a person of some learning.

The content of the meeting is what the client says, what he does not say when he would be expected to say something, and what he does, when his actions convey a feeling or attitude. A statement of a problem does not yield a prescription for dealing with it, nor medicine to relieve sadness or tension, but an examination of it and of how the client has handled it in the past and proposes to handle it in the future. This meeting lasts close to an hour, and it occurs at least once a week for a year or more. This is what many professional therapists think of as psychotherapy.

However, there are endless variations on this basic model, and it is necessary to present some concept of their range if for no other reason than to demonstrate that certain attributes, for example, duration, which have been used to distinguish psychotherapy are not definitive. In this chapter the variables associated with the meeting itself will be examined by means of the following plan:

1. What has been varied and how it has been varied will be pointed out and illustrated. The intent is not to present every variation, but to specify the scope of variation. Particular attention will be given to any research evidence that favors any practice or technique.

2. Research possibilities will be noted.

3. The implications of the analysis of these variables for the definition of psychotherapy will be discussed.

A similar plan will be followed in subsequent chapters. Now let us begin with the setting in which the meeting between therapist and client usually takes place, the therapist's office.

VARYING THE SETTING

In contrast to the therapist's office of today, which almost without exception is in some clinic, hospital, institution, or professional building, the office of Sigmund Freud was located in his home. Undoubtedly his wife and children were not unnoticed by his patients, nor, indeed, was any attempt made to conceal them. During his early practice in psychoanalysis, Freud might even invite a patient to have dinner with his family, and in his later years, though he now was more keenly aware of the need for a certain degree of detachment, he was still agreeable to the serving of refreshments from time to time (Jones, 1958, p. 230).

Freud's office would probably seem a bit garish to many people. It was rich in the details of his personal preferences and interests and was loaded, cluttered is not too strong a term, with objets d'art. There were pictures, figurines, sculpture, and pottery in profusion. Many of these were Egyptian, Greek, and Assyrian antiquities, and they testified that here was a man with a passion for the past. Not only were there oriental rugs on the floor, but also on the famous couch, on a table, and hanging on the walls (Jones, 1955). This was a room that proclaimed with pride and warmth the personality of its owner.

Although such an office may be too opulent for modern tastes, the question might well be raised as to why there should be a need for the relative blandness of the therapists' rooms of today. In large measure the discovery by Breuer and Freud that the patient might transfer feelings to the analyst that were appropriately directed toward parental figures is given as a reason. It is assumed that by being discrete about his own preferences and dislikes, the therapist remains unknown, a kind of blank screen on which the client can project his emotions and attitudes. Moreover, so long as the therapist's personality is unobtrusive, he retains an excellent position from which to point out the unreasonableness of certain feelings that the client may experience toward him. Essentially, the therapist wishes to avoid giving his client any justification for having these feelings, and hence, as Wolberg suggests (1967, p. 438), the decorative plan should not be "too outlandish."

Nevertheless, there has never been any study that has demonstrated a need for austerity. On the contrary, there is a considerable body of folklore and advertising to suggest that the quality of an office denotes the status of its occupant. A name on the door not only cries for carpeting on the floor, as the magazine ads tells us repeatedly, but also speaks within our culture of permanence and prestige.

In particular, the size of a room is equated implicitly with its costliness and the authority and status of its user. It is common knowledge, conveyed by the mass media, that a small office contains a person of little importance while a large office is occupied by someone with high status and responsibility. Thus humor can be introduced into any cinematic or theatrical presentation by presenting a bumbling, incompetent individual behind a large desk in a choicely appointed office.

Further, it is known that: "*Who* says something is usually as important as *what* is said in the determination of the impact of a communication" (Hovland, 1954). Accordingly, it would be expected that, all other things being equal, a therapist in an office of sizable proportions and attractive furnishings would promote greater confidence in his competence and would be thought to be more effective, at least in the early stages of treatment, than the therapist who sees his clients in a "closet."

To date there has been only one study that has experimentally explored this issue. Kasmar, Griffin, and Mauritzen (1968) had two third-year psychiatric residents see 115 outpatient adults for initial interviews. These interviews took place in one of two rooms, designated by the investigators as "beautiful" and "ugly." The beautiful room had a carpet, a plant, an abstract painting on the wall, and it was clean and neat. The ugly room had asphalt tiles on the floor, was devoid of decorations, and looked sloppy. Unfortunately, both of the rooms were windowless and 6×8 ft in size, dimensions which in almost anyone's frame of reference are modest and quite unimpressive. A beautiful office of that size speaks less of authority than of a valiant effort to preserve one's dignity under trying circumstances. Not too surprisingly, then, although the patients rated the ugly room less favorably than they did the beautiful one, their impressions of their own moods and their evaluations of their therapist did not seem to be related to the office in which they were seen. Surely this study deserves to be repeated, but with a beautiful room that is larger, a minimum of 10×12 ft being more in keeping with the size of an office, than the one that is ugly.

Of late there has been great interest in the setting, conceived of in the broad perspective of a neighborhood, building, or institution, and one might even profitably consider the times in which we live. When thought of within such a context, the issue of the setting clearly emerges as less a matter of psychotherapy itself than of the variables that alter its effectiveness and availability.

As a general rule, it has been found that whatever makes it easier for the client to make use of psychotherapy increases the likelihood that the client will make use of this service. For example, the setting up of clinics or service agencies within the neighborhoods of target populations, rather than compelling the clients to travel by car or public transportation for help, brings about an increase in the numbers of persons within those neighborhoods who make use of the clinic or agency (Nahemow, 1968). The result is that it has become somewhat debatable whether "hard to reach" should be applied to clients or service organizations.

In addition, it has been demonstrated that mental hospitals may promote and perpetuate psychotic behavior. Without intentionally doing so, members of the staff may reward or reinforce bizarre verbalizations (Ayllon and Haughton, 1964), or the institution itself may have procedures that frustrate those patients who strive for independence while favoring those who profess weakness (Towbin, 1969). Of course if antitherapeutic forces were discovered to be at work in the institution, the aim would be to help the staff to become aware of what they were doing that was at cross-purposes with their goal of restoring persons to a useful, productive life.

Despite the significance of this work, this discussion of settings serves mainly to make it evident that there is nothing definitive about where psychotherapy is conducted. It can be practiced in almost any location, although where it is offered can make the difference in whether or not it is accepted and used. The office has no special furnishings or equipment, no particular characteristics that make it uniquely suitable for psychotherapy. Therefore, while further studies may suggest manipulations of variables in the setting that would enhance the effectiveness of treatment, it is necessary to look elsewhere to other variables for what is definitive.

VARYING THE HOUR

Robert Lindner's book *The Fifty-Minute Hour* informed the public by its title that when therapists speak of a treatment "hour," they do not wish to be taken literally. The "hour" varies from place to place, and even from therapist to therapist within the same place. Freud's "hour" was 55 minutes. In many clinics and hospitals it is 50 minutes. In some settings it is 45 minutes. Only one thing seems fairly certain about the "hour"; rarely is it 60 minutes.

The reason for this departure from the world standard is eminently practical and sensible. Because appointments customarily are scheduled to begin on the hour, there is afforded an interval of from five to fifteen minutes when the therapist may jot down notes, make telephone calls, attend to his correspondence, confer with colleagues, and perhaps just relax. This period of time is mainly for his benefit, although it seems reasonable to suppose that it may save him from exhaustion and thus be of some indirect value to those clients he sees later in his day.

Of course there is nothing sacrosanct about the 45 to 55 minute hour, and it happens that psychotherapy does occur in longer and shorter sessions. Ziferstein (1966) has reported that within the Soviet Union psychiatrists gear the length of their meetings to what they believe are the needs of the particular case. Accordingly, their interviews may be of any duration, and although they tend to be on the relatively short side, they vary for the most part from 30 minutes to two hours.

At the other end of the continuum, it is not unusual to find practitioners who believe that there can be psychotherapy in the brief exchanges that take place on hospital wards when the patient is asked about his condition. Nor is it rare for therapists to report that there are moments of great intensity, incidents when a single remark or action had an enormous effect on the client and his progress.

Group therapy meetings, as a rule, last longer than sessions for an individual, and ordinarily run anywhere from 60 to 90 minutes. The reason for the added time, according to group therapists, is to insure that each member of the group has an opportunity for participation, and also it takes longer for the group to warm up and get going than it does for an individual.

Marathon groups (Bach, 1967) have recently been developed and have aroused much interest both among the public and professionals. Their major distinction is that they fully exploit the variable of time. They last from 24 to 48 practically continuous hours, and are deliberately made so long that the grinding effects of increasing fatigue and the pressures of confinement will irritate the group members and will provoke them to honest, intimate, straightforward appraisals of themselves and one another. It is an innovation which has quickly gained a measure of popularity, but which provides a great temptation to extrapolate it into the absurd.

Conceivably, a psychotherapeutic meeting could last as little as a few seconds to as long as the life span of the client. Yet practically there are limits which narrow the variability considerably. On the one hand, even if clients were perfectly willing to do whatever was asked of them, the therapist's endurance, needs, and obligations to himself, to his clients, and to his family set restrictions on the duration of appointments. On the other hand, there are questions about the meaning of time to the client.

In this culture the passage of time is associated with a number of variables that bear no necessary relationship to it. One recognizes correctly that "time is money," it has value, and one should expect to pay for a service roughly in proportion to the amount of time it takes. Yet people have also come to learn, and the mass media tell them repeatedly, that time is a measure of:

1. The importance of a meeting; important meetings last longer than unimportant ones.
2. The thoroughness and excellence of a piece of work; a good job takes longer than a poor one.
3. The esteem of one person for another; if you like someone, you spend more time with him than you do with someone you don't like.
4. The seriousness, severity, and difficulty of a problem; operations and deliberations of long duration suggest matters of great complexity and gravity.

Obviously, the duration of an appointment can have meanings other than those intended. It may convey to the client information about the severity of his problem, about whether he is valued by his therapist, and about the competence of the helping person. Long appointments may enhance the client's self-esteem and feelings of worth, but they may also suggest that the condition is difficult to modify. Short appointments may be reassuring because they indicate that the problem is not too serious and that it should respond readily to help, but they may also say that the therapist does not feel that the client is worthy of too much bother.

Further, what is "long" and "short" are relative matters. Some clients, especially those who assume that an "hour" is 60 minutes, may feel that they have been "shortchanged" when the therapist announces at ten minutes to the hour, "Well, our time is up." Other clients may be uncomfortable from their first appointment to their last because they are unable to talk about themselves for an entire session. Therefore, the same 50 minutes may in one case be insulting and in another case be burdensome.

But, it may be argued, a psychotherapy session has to be 45 or 50 or 55 minutes. Why? A search for evidence discloses that there is none to support the use of any specific duration for the treatment interview. The entire question seems to have been decided on the basis of custom, personal preference, or common practice in a particular setting. When one pauses for a moment to reflect that thousands of "hours" each year are given to individual psychotherapy, that the professional time available for this service is precious, and that there is no empirical reason for the session not being 20 or 25 minutes instead of 45 or 50, the potential for greater usefulness to the public seems dazzling. How might this potential be tapped?

It is possible that the best interests of the client and the demands for economy can both be served by a very simple technique. Rather than routinely inform the client of how many minutes he will receive, and then perhaps deal with his feelings of disappointment or apprehension, he could be asked during the first meeting for his understanding or expectations about the length of the interview. In many cases the client will more likely than not have an expectation that corresponds with what is practiced; for this the mass media can be thanked since they have given the subject some publicity. Still, the probability is high that there will be clients whose expectations will be "unrealistic"; some may ask for more time than the therapist is willing to give, and others may ask for less time than the therapist believes is required in order to be of help; or there may be many who will insist that they have no opinion at all on the matter. Under these circumstances it could be explained quite reasonably that the need to be of service to other clients or the proper performance of the method of treatment make necessary a maximum and minimum duration, let us say at the most 50 minutes and at the least 25.

By a negotiation of this kind, no more time would be offered to a client than is ordinarily given, and there could be many instances in which time is saved. The author investigated the acceptability of this suggestion by asking a group of middle-class women (N = 125) and a group of students in introductory psychology (N = 149) if they would like a psychotherapist who "discussed with the client setting-up a reasonable time for their appointments, making them 30 minutes, perhaps, rather than 50." It should be noted that the question was phrased deliberately in a negative manner, in the direction of reducing time. Nevertheless, 61% of the women and 52% of the students stated that they would prefer a therapist who would do this, indicating that a sizable number of people would favor such a procedure.

At the very least, the technique would turn what is now usually an arbitrary arrangement into an occasion for involving the client in the planning of his treatment and in the assessing of his condition. Moreover, the therapist's indication of a willingness to be responsive to his client's feelings and needs about the appointments, his display of flexibility, and his immediate sharing of responsibility may well be expected to have salutary effects.

The need for research in this area is evident. It is also obvious that even if there were a specific duration for the treatment interview, which as has been seen there is not, it would not help to define psychotherapy since meetings of similar duration occur in many other contexts.

VARYING THE FREQUENCY

The term "frequency" refers to the number of psychotherapy interviews over a given period, for example, once a week. The frequency can range from as often as three times a day, in certain cases of intensive analyses with psychotics, to as seldom as once every month or so, when the aim is to maintain the adjustment of some chronic patient. Even this brief remark suggests that the objectives or goals of the treatment have a bearing on the frequency.

The method of treatment and custom also play a major role in the determination of the frequency. For example, during the early development of psychoanalysis in Europe, a client might be seen six times a week. However, for some unexplained reason, perhaps economy, analysts in the United States reduced the frequency to five times a week, and then to three times a week or less (Frank, 1961, p. 14). Traditionally, however, psychoanalysis as a "deep," reconstructive procedure is associated with frequencies of three or more visits per week, while other methods of psychotherapy attempt to achieve their goals on a frequency of once or twice a week, with the weekly meeting being the most prevalent schedule offered.

Because there can be so much variation in frequency and because the corresponding investment by both the therapist and client can be so markedly different, a great deal has been written about this subject in an attempt to provide guidelines for making decisions. Wolberg (1967, p. 510) has presented an excellent summary of the thinking about this matter.

He suggests that more frequent visits are indicated:

1. During periods of crisis or when the client is showing signs of disorganizing anxiety, depression, and confusion.
2. When a dependent or more intense relationship is desired.
3. With clients who are hostile, rigid, or very resistant to treatment.
4. If a client is impulsive and requires the therapist as a constant check on his antisocial or self-destructive tendencies.

Indications for less frequent visits are:

1. When a dependent or intense relationship is not desired.
2. During periods of stability in clients whose conditions are chronic.
3. With clients who seek to use the treatment primarily as a means to escape from the responsibility of having to deal with immediate real life problems.
4. Where a tapering-off of the therapy is indicated.

These, then, are some of the guidelines on frequency. They state, in the main, that the intensity of the relationship is positively related to the frequency, and they urge that during emergencies the client be seen more often.

In practice, however, there is usually not much opportunity to respond to these signs for frequency change. The policies of a clinic or institution tend to be utilitarian, that is, based on a conscientious desire to reach as many clients as possible rather than to invest professional time heavily for the welfare of a few. Accordingly, it is understood that although there is some provision made for more frequent visits, appointments are to be scheduled on a once a week basis. Moreover, the temptation to depart from this schedule fades under the pressures and demands for service, while there is little research that one could marshal in favor of seeing clients two or three times a week. Thus the frequency is apt to be a function of custom, expediency, and compromise, rather than a flexible adjustment to the apparent needs of a particular case.

Although therapists believe that more frequent visits are related to a more intensive form of treatment, there is no claim for its relation to the duration of treatment. For example, no one seriously argues that a person seen in analysis twice a week for two years could have attained similar results by being seen four times a week for a year. In a similar vein, Frank (1961, p. 14) has noted that the length of an analysis does not seem to depend upon whether the analysand is seen three or five times a week. Instead, what is significant in determining the duration of the analysis is the analyst's opinion about how long it should be in order for it to be effective. That this should be a matter of opinion is hardly surprising in view of the meagre evidence that can be brought to bear on this issue.

One of the most ambitious studies lends little encouragement to those who wish to promote one frequency over another. It does suggest, however, that there is a lower limit of frequency below which psychotherapy is ineffective in producing any marked changes.

Fifty-four white, neurotic, mostly female patients were assigned at random to three psychiatrists (Imber et al., 1957; Frank, 1961, pp. 208–213). Each psychiatrist saw about an equal number of these patients under one of three conditions: individual therapy for one hour a week; group therapy for 1½ hours a week; and, in what was intended to be a minimal amount of therapy, individual sessions lasting not more than ½ hour every two weeks.

None of the patients was seen in treatment for longer than six months. Evaluations of their conditions were made before psychotherapy began, after six months, and after one, two, and five years, an unusually extensive and, as shall soon be seen, highly informative follow-up period.

One of the interesting findings was that about half the patients obtained help of some kind from others, not only during the follow-up, but during the time they were being seen in therapy as well. This convincingly demonstrated that it would be a grave mistake to regard the helping process as confined to the therapist's office. Beyond that it suggests that many patients feel a need for assistance that is so strong that it is not satisfied by a once a week appointment. Or it could also be that the constructive experiences of psychotherapy encourage the person to make use of help wherever he can find it.

Perhaps the most significant result of the study was that, in general, all the patients appeared to be functioning better at the five-year follow-up than they did when they were seen at six months. This led Frank (1961, p. 213) to speculate that frequency and maybe even psychotherapy itself are eventually of little consequence. After all, patients under all three conditions experienced some immediate relief of distress. And while at six months those in the minimal therapy group had improved least in the area of social effectiveness (behaviors such as overdependence and aggressiveness which are disruptive to satisfactory interpersonal relationships), the differences were not pronounced after five years. Frank supposed that in neurotic disorders a recovery process may operate, which can be accelerated by psychotherapy, but which is not blocked if professional treatment is not available.

This conclusion may have to be modified because of findings that came to light when the patients were followed up ten years after their formal treatment had ended (Imber et al., 1968). By that time only 34 of the original sample could be located, a "loss" of about a third of the group. The patients who had been seen in the minimal treatment condition were now judged to be significantly worse than the others in social effectiveness, although not in personal discomfort, a situation that had prevailed at the six-month, but not at the five-year, follow-up.

There are problems in making too much of these results because of the attrition of the sample and because of the inconsistencies in the data over time. It is possible to be impressed by the finding that differences between the groups could be detected ten years after the treatment had ended, and it is possible to be unimpressed because significant differences were not found on all measures. Probably it is most prudent to suppose that psychotherapy can have salubrious effects, particularly in the sphere of social relations, although these effects do not always seem to investigators to be commensurate with the effort and expense involved.

A similar conclusion was reached by Sheperd, Oppenheim, and Mitchell (1966) following their study of 50 children who had been seen in therapy in a child guidance clinic in Great Britain. These youngsters were compared with a matched sample of 50 children who exhibited similar problems as the treated group, but whose parents had not referred them for help. (It must be noted that one-fourth of the children in the child guidance clinic population had disturbances that were so severe that they could not be matched in the general population.)

After about two years following the conclusion of treatment all the children were evaluated, and it was found that the percent of improvement in each group was approximately the same (65% in the treated versus 61% in the untreated group). Since the problems and outcomes were similar, the investigators wondered why one child was referred while another was not. They discovered that the major reason was that the mothers differed. Those mothers who referred their children tended to be anxious, depressed, easily upset, and concerned about the seriousness of the problem and their inability to deal with it; the other mothers, however, regarded the same problem behavior as a temporary trouble, which was likely to be outgrown without professional intervention.

Although it was not specifically studied, it is likely that here too psychotherapy accelerated the recovery process. Moreover, it was demonstrated that since treatment was helpful in reducing parental concern, it was not without some benefit. Nevertheless, the findings by Sheperd and his colleagues are disappointing to those who wish for something dramatic. They suggest that psychotherapy is valuable, but in the majority of cases with children not essential, in order to bring about constructive changes. As expressed by Sheperd, Oppenheim, and Mitchell: ". . . many so-called disturbances of behaviour are no more than temporary exaggerations of widely distributed reaction patterns."

The findings of these studies may seem to lend support to the notion that a frequency of no appointments a week is a sensible plan. After all, some might argue, if the eventual outcomes are about the same between treated and untreated groups, why bother with the trouble and expense of treatment? This question is partially answered by the results of the studies themselves: the acceleration of the process and the feeling of comfort derived from doing something and having something done about a problem. That these benefits are by no means trifling can be appreciated when it is considered that people are willing to pay a premium in order to arrive at a destination by a means of travel that is faster and more comfortable than another.

Moreover, the next two studies that will be mentioned suggest that when the outcome is examined carefully, differences between groups can be observed that are consistent with the Imber et al. study. Lorr et al. (1962) based their research on the treatment of 133 Veterans Administration outpatients who had been randomly assigned to be seen once a week, twice a week, and once every other week. Regardless of the frequency, at first there seemed to be little difference in the outcome. However, when the patients in the twice a week group who had a high number of interviews (mean = 62, range 43–96) were compared with those in the once every other week group who had a low number of interviews (mean = 29, range 17–42), it was found that the former described themselves as more assertive, outspoken, and independent, that is, in the social effectiveness area in which differences were found by Imber et al. Although the investigators supposed that within a given period the number of interviews is more important in effecting constructive changes than is the frequency, the data are really not that clear. It is quite possible that the patients in the low frequency group were less able and less inclined to profit from therapy on their rather skimpy schedule of assistance.

The second study is rather unusual because it compared a group of young boys seen in analytic therapy four times a week with a group seen once a week. Unfortunately there were only four children in each group so that the findings must be regarded with caution. While there were no pronounced differences in the evaluations of the two groups at the end of treatment, a year later it was found that the boys who had been seen more frequently had continued to make gains, while those who had been seen once a week had advanced little in their psychological development and achievement in reading (Heinicke et al., 1965). These results suggest that some of the effects of intensive psychotherapy may not be evident at the termination of treatment, but only become apparent afterward. Hence follow-up is crucial in assessing the effectiveness of psychotherapy, as has certainly been seen, not only in this study, but in the dampening outcomes of the investigations by Sheperd and Imber.

Admittedly, the experimental evidence about frequency is meagre. Yet what little there is does join with impressions gained in the practice of psychotherapy to make one strongly suspect that a frequency of less than once a week is not going to be very productive of significant personality change, at least under ordinary circumstances. This qualification must be added because situations are possible where a low frequency, or no frequency at all, can be in the best interests of the client. For example, Scher (1961) described two clients who had already completed several courses of psychotherapy, without notable success, and who were ready to begin yet another treatment program. By persistently *not* seeing them, Scher believed he set in motion a process which enabled his patients to face their problems squarely and to effect their own improvement. Therefore, it would seem that a reduction in frequency or a low frequency can serve to spur some clients to independence by communicating the message to them that the therapist believes they can "go it alone."

Evidently the practice of psychotherapy has leaped ahead of its empirical justification, and no one really knows whether it is essential for clients to be seen more than once or twice a week. Yet here too, as was the case with the "hour," it would seem reasonable to ask the client his opinion about what he would believe to be an appropriate schedule of treatment. His expectations may lead the therapist to raise or lower the frequency he might otherwise have offered, and most likely would provide useful information to assess the meaning of the schedule to the client, a meaning that often is just not considered.

Further, it is clear that the frequency is not definitive of psychotherapy, nor for that matter is the duration, which has been alleged to be distinctive and which shall be discussed next.

VARYING THE DURATION

How long the treatment should last has been a topic for contention for many years, particularly in psychoanalytic circles where the guideposts for termination can be somewhat ambiguous. Freud's position on this matter is both classic and still sensible (Freud, 1959). He recognized that the issue could be viewed from the standpoints of ideals, practicality, and reality. Ideally, the analyst might like to see the person remain in therapy until he had achieved standards of perfection in his functioning which would seem to insure his happiness and productivity. Practically, the termination of treatment can be allowed to take place when the patient feels better, even though the therapist may still see deficiencies in the personality and the likelihood of problems and setbacks. In reality professionals are aware that the work of psychotherapy never really ends and that the person will struggle throughout his life to increase his understanding of himself.

This discussion will be confined to the question of duration from the standpoint of practicality. However, this is not as clear-cut as might have been thought from Freud's comment. What makes the issue so debatable is that psychotherapists differ among themselves in their ways of looking at human behavior, hence in how willing they are to accept the client at his word when he claims to be feeling better. By no stretch of the imagination should this be construed as trivial or frivolous. For many psychotherapists the matter is one of acting responsibly and extending themselves to their clients, despite the prospect of experiencing personal inconveniences.

Let us try to make the subject more real by imagining that we have before us a client who has completed three months of psychotherapy. A person who had felt depressed for no apparent reason, he now tells us that almost immediately after his treatment began there was an alleviation of his symptom, improvement in his work, and renewed interest in social activities. He is pleased with his progress, impressed by the skill of the therapist, even though he confesses that he is still unaware of what upset and distressed him, and curious about whether the course of psychotherapy can stop. What should the therapist say and do?

According to some therapists, this client has recovered; his condition has been treated by them and cured. They would feel satisfaction in a job well done, and they would end the treatment with no misgivings.

Other therapists would not be too sure of what had been accomplished. However, they would decide that since the client had evaluated his present circumstances in a reasonable manner and had come to the conclusion that the appointments should stop, they would go along with his doing just that.

But to many of their colleagues, especially to those among them of an analytic orientation, these practices would seem unwise and in contradiction with what is needed. The client would appear, in their opinion, to be resisting treatment by a "flight into health." They would see his recovery as a defense, and they would question and cause him to question the soundness of his decision. Thus the very same situation is often perceived and handled by different therapists in ways that are both quite different and quite consequential for the client.

The duration of psychotherapy can and does vary with the method employed, and these variations are based on fundamental disagreements about the nature of man and about how best he can be helped. What is sensible practice for one professional may impress another as naiveté or tragic foolishness. There are therapists who believe that important and far-reaching changes can take place in a person's attitudes and behavior within the space of a single interview (Alexander and French, 1946; Saul, 1951; May, Angel, and Ellenberger, 1958). They would argue that in a moment there can occur a "meaningful encounter" or a "critical incident" which can significantly alter the individual's personality for the better. They can see a word of praise, a suggestion, a bit of advice, a sign of trust and confidence at just the right time as setting the person off on a new course in life. With such therapists the duration could be marvelously brief.

Their attitude is a most optimistic one, and it emphasizes and exalts the flexibility of man. They tend to see people as responsive to change, as amenable to compromise, and as capable of starting anew. Although they recognize that neurotics, the emotionally disturbed, the maladjusted are limited in this capacity, as evidenced by their persistence in their self-defeating patterns of behavior, they are inclined to be more impressed by the interval between repetitions of symptoms than by the repetitions themselves.

In contrast, there are therapists who see man as handicapped in his ability to modify himself because of internal forces of which he is not fully aware. They are struck by the rigidity, by the compulsivity, by the stubbornness with which people will cling to their symptoms. Again and again they have heard clients make constructive plans, and then observed them to act in opposition to their good intentions. Their clinical experiences have convinced them that long-term psychotherapy, the longer the better, is the best and most certain method for bringing about lasting gains.

This point of view, one that sees disturbed behavior as tenacious re-capitulations of conflicts, was quite prevalent in the United States during the 1940s and 1950s. At that time a sizable research investment was made in order to predict which clients were likely to remain in treatment and which were likely to "drop out" or "defect" after a few sessions. It was generally agreed that those clients who terminated "prematurely" were a deplorable waste of professional time and effort. Therefore it made sense to search for criteria that would enable them to be identified, and then either removed from the usual treatment process or helped, or prepared for help, in some other way.

What tended to be overlooked was that defection had taken place from the therapist's point of view, but not necessarily from the client's. His premature departure may have been a resistance to abandoning his unconscious conflicts, but it also may have been prompted by rational, legitimate reasons, of which one may have been the alleviation of his distressing symptoms. Accordingly, the "dropout" differed from the client who remained in treatment not only in the fact that he did not receive a "full course" of psychotherapy, but presumably also in that his felt need for this service was less.

Nevertheless, "terminator" and "remainer" were treated as differing in only one important respect in a number of studies that evaluated the effectiveness of psychotherapy; the latter completed the treatment that had been prescribed, while the former did not. Thus it was expected that the "terminators" would be found to be less satisfactorily adjusted than the "treated" group. But to the surprise and disappointment of psychotherapists, it was found instead that the outcomes for those who "defected" and those who remained were similar (Eysenck, 1961).

Although a number of plausible explanations were offered for these unexpected findings, one that gained wide currency was that many clients in the "untreated" group had recovered "spontaneously." The term "spontaneously" was understood to mean that a variety of factors may have acted in one case or another to bring about a remission of symptoms. It was suggested that perhaps a few of these clients had discussed their problems with ministers, friends of the family, or had mulled them over alone, and by such a method had diminished their anxiety and had made solutions more possible. Some were thought to have had a corrective emotional experience or to have met with success, for example, a delightful vacation or a longed-for promotion. Or it may have been that for a number there had been a fortunate change in status so that now they received greater respect, affection, and signs of approval from their environment than they had obtained heretofore. It could even have been that in some cases new persons had come into their lives with whom they could identify and whose behavior they could emulate, or new situations had been brought about by a birth or by a death which removed pressures and made different and healthy reactions appropriate (Stevenson, 1961). Really, anything was possible. As Bergin summarized the thinking on this matter: ". . . the studies reviewed appear to have demonstrated that control groups may actually represent a test of the effectiveness of no professional therapeutic conditions" (Bergin, 1963).

Nevertheless, whatever the reasons for these positive changes among those who did not continue and complete their course of psychotherapy, that constructive changes could occur "spontaneously" was widely recognized, and it made personality seem less fixed and rigid than had been thought. Clients were now regarded as more resilient and adaptable than before, and it did not seem so farfetched to expect some of them to profit from a brief period of psychotherapy (Wolberg, 1965), particularly when the treatment was offered during a time of crisis in the individual's life (Waldfogel and Gardner, 1961). In fact the belief grew that under certain circumstances psychotherapy of a short duration might be preferable to long-term treatment.

Undoubtedly the arbitrariness that frequently enters into the length of therapy has played a role in making professionals responsive to manipulating the duration. It is difficult to maintain that treatment has to last a specific period of time when one considers that psychoanalyses can vary from one to six years, depending on the age and training of the analyst and, apparently, on the geographical location in which the analysis takes place (Frank, 1961, pp. 14, 15). Furthermore, the research that has been done does not point to a significant relationship between improvement and the duration of treatment (Stieper and Wiener, 1959).

Mensh and Golden (1951) found that of 352 veterans who had benefited from therapy, about half had been helped in less than five interviews. Similarly, Garfield and Kurz (1952) in their study of 1216 cases referred to a mental hygiene clinic reported that almost half the patients who were thought to have improved had less than ten sessions. However, since these studies were done after the fact, they are suspect because the less seriously disturbed clients may have been seen less often. More convincing demonstrations of the effectiveness of short-term psychotherapy can be based on the investigations of Muench (1965) and Shlien, Mosak, and Dreikurs (1962). This last bit of research shall be presented in some detail.

Shlien and his colleagues sought to compare the effectiveness of Adlerian and Rogerian therapies, and also to contrast results obtained by seeing clients twice a week for 20 interviews versus seeing clients for an unlimited period of time. For their measure of progress, they employed the degree of correspondence between how the person rated himself on certain adjectives (Self concept) and how he indicated he would like to be (Ideal Self concept). (The extent to which the two ratings agree gives a measure of how satisfied the person is with himself.) Earlier studies by Rogers and Dymond (1954) had demonstrated that this agreement between Self and Ideal Self ratings increases during treatment, and that for college students, at least, the closer the degree of this correspondence, the better are social and work adjustments (Turner and Vanderlippe, 1958).

When the ratings were analyzed, no significant differences were found between the clients who had been seen in Adlerian and Rogerian psychotherapy. This was not too surprising. What was impressive was that the time-limited-interview clients had magnitudes of correlation between their Self and Ideal Self ratings that were very similar to those that were obtained at the conclusion of unlimited therapy; this despite the fact that the unlimited group had an average of 37 interviews, or almost twice as many as the time-limited group. Moreover, by the end of only seven interviews in the time-limited group, the correlation between their ratings had reached its maximum, that is, they seemed to progress at an accelerated pace. It seemed clear that clients can change appreciably in their attitudes about themselves in a short period of time.

All of this should be a little reassuring to therapists, since they know all too well that brief therapy has been, albeit unintentionally, what most clients in clinics receive. Mensh and Golden (1951) and Garfield and Kurz (1952) reported 85% and 91%, respectively, of their samples had less than ten interviews. For a variety of reasons, the great majority of those who apply to clinics and counseling centers wind up being seen briefly.

Some clients are assumed to terminate contacts because they experience a genuine relief of symptoms or an improvement in the situation that prompted their request for service. Others perhaps have second thoughts and decide that their problems are relatively minor, or at least not worth the trouble of trying to solve them. Undoubtedly, waiting lists and clinic procedures take their toll by discouraging and infuriating others

(Ginott et al., 1959). It is also known that clients of low socioeconomic status tend not to remain in treatment for long, whether because therapists do not respond to them as favorably as they do to middle- and upper-class clients or because of idiosyncrasies of their own.

Further, the suggestibility of the client also is relevant in determining the duration. Imber and his colleagues (1956) found that patients who responded positively to suggestions that they were swaying were inclined to remain in therapy longer, for four or more interviews, than those who did not. While the group that was discovered to be the most likely to reject or terminate therapy abruptly was made up of lower-class patients who did not sway. Consistent with these findings is Schroeder's (1960) report that clients who believed strongly that they were responsible for their behavior (lower-class clients tend to believe their behavior is controlled by external forces and events) had a longer duration and got more from their counseling than clients who did not.

The therapist also can wittingly and unwittingly act to affect the duration. He may make use of an assortment of techniques that are known to reduce the length of treatment. He can negotiate with the client for a limit on the number of months, or interviews, that treatment will take, a procedure popularized by Otto Rank. He can use hypnosis, as in hypnoanalysis, hypnotherapy, and reciprocal inhibition; drugs, such as sodium amytal, sodium pentothal, and more recently LSD (Abramson, 1967); all in order to reduce inhibitions, lessen resistances, and make "repressed" material accessible to awareness, thus abbreviating the course of therapy.

Moreover, the therapist's attitudes about diagnostic categories, treatment goals, and the modifiability of people play a part in his expectation of how long psychotherapy should last. Many therapists expect that psychoses and character disorders, in general those disturbances that are severe, chronic, and distinguished by a history of failure and rejection, will be especially time-consuming. However, they would predict that persons who have mild or acute situational disorders and who have experienced some degree of accomplishment and success will be tractable. These attitudes are related to the goals that they set for treatment. The relief of symptoms, as a goal, is associated with brief psychotherapy and usually accompanies the belief that the alleviation of disturbance will be sufficient to allow the client to feel relatively happy and well. A reconstruction of personality functioning is considered a long term goal, and it is thought to be essential by most psychoanalysts when treating certain psychoneurotic disorders.

Although we shall have more to say about the personality characteristics of the therapist in Chapter 4, his loquaciousness and degree of activity are among those unwitting attributes that appear to affect the client in such a way that they eventually affect the duration, that is, therapists who are taciturn have longer treatments than those who are talkative and zestful (Aldrich, 1967). Now when all this information is put together, it leads to the prediction that therapy of brief duration is most likely to occur when an active, talkative therapist has as his goal the alleviation of anxiety in a submissive, suggestible client.

What more does this analysis tell about the duration of treatment? Clearly that it is not always determined by the nature of the disturbance alone. On the contrary, there is much evidence to suggest that frequently the therapist, with his beliefs, methods, and concerns about prophylaxis, plays a decisive role in determining how long treatment will last. His subtle convictions about his own omnipotence and his opinions about his clients' flexibility or capacity for positive change are of importance not only to those he treats, but also to the larger community of which he is a member. For it is obvious that psychotherapy of short duration would be an economic saving since it would enable many more persons to be seen by a given staff of mental health professionals.

A belief in man's flexibility, in his capacity to change for the better, would seem to be crucial to the therapist's confidence in the efficacy of psychotherapy of brief duration. This belief, in the absence of any name, can be called *anthropomeliorism*, and it would seem to be of some importance to the course, duration, and effectiveness of psychotherapy to assess the compatibility of client and therapist on this variable.

Finally, it can be concluded that there is nothing specific about the duration of psychotherapy that would be of help in its definition.

CONCLUSIONS

The setting, the hour, the frequency, and the duration of psychotherapy are not definitive for this method of treatment. Further, these variables appear to be more functions of custom, convenience, and conviction than of any substantial body of research. Yet what little evidence there is offers no support for the assumption that therapists are not guided by their theories in their decisions concerning psychotherapy, and at the same time argues for openness to possible modifications as new evidence becomes available. In any situation where the treatment of individuals is not individualized, there are bound to be instances of injustice. Therapists must recognize what influences they bring to bear in their decisions on these matters of time. It is their own beliefs, which they are able to impose upon their clients, that are of great consequence to their clients and their profession.

CHAPTER 3

Manipulations of the Participants in Psychotherapy

Everything great in the world comes from neurotics. They alone have founded our religions and composed our masterpieces. Never will the world know all it owes to them nor all they have suffered to enrich us. We enjoy lovely music, beautiful paintings, a thousand intellectual delicacies, but we have no idea of their cost to those who invented them, in sleepless nights, tears, spasmodic laughter, rashes, asthmas, epilepsies, and the fear of death, which is worst than all the rest.

Marcel Proust

The practice of psychotherapy requires people, but the only people who are absolutely essential to its practice are clients. If that fact is kept firmly in mind, some of the innovations that recently have been proposed can be better appreciated. And that is largely what shall be considered in this chapter, new techniques that are intended to help the client.

Some of the techniques may seem impractical; probably some of them are impractical. However, all of them were suggested by serious professionals who found them instructive and helpful. One purpose in examining them is to illustrate what has been done, to note what could be done, and to show just how varied is this method of treatment called psychotherapy. Such an examination should serve further to make clear why the definitions that have specified a relationship between *a* therapist and *a* client are unacceptable, and it should give an indication of the variability that must be encompassed by a definition that is satisfactory.

The basic model of psychotherapy is the therapist seeing a client, and the two of them communicating. That is what is meant by individual psychotherapy, and it is what most people envision when they conceive of psychological treatment. However, many changes have been proposed in the number of both participants, to the extent of reducing the number of therapists to zero. Let us consider the possible variations in the number of therapists first.

VARYING THE NUMBER OF THERAPISTS

It is possible to dispense quickly with the recommendations that involve more than one therapist to a client. The shortage of professionals sees to it that they are seldom put into practice and thus that they arouse little popular enthusiasm.

In multiple therapy there are at least two therapists, often one male and one female in order to represent father and mother figures, and usually one client. This arrangement is supposed to increase the likelihood of transference reactions, hence to make it easier to get into the conflicted relationships that the client had with his parents. Even when the two therapists are of the same sex, it is thought likely that the client will distort the characteristics of one of them into those of the parental figure of the other sex, that is, he will eventually regard one therapist as maternal and one as paternal. Multiple therapy is commended for several additional advantages it possesses: two therapists are apt to reduce the intensity of resistances and negative transference; by discussing the client while in his company, the therapists can impart insights to him; and the method serves as an excellent means for the training of one therapist or the other, or both (Dreikurs, 1950).

Theoretically, there is no limit on the number of therapists who could be employed to represent members of the family constellation and other significant persons in the client's life. From time to time more than two therapists are utilized in this fashion in the practice of psychodrama, although for the most part nonprofessionals are recruited from the audience to play various roles. Nevertheless, as was mentioned earlier, it is impractical to advocate procedures requiring two or more therapists to a client when there are many more clients waiting to be seen than therapists available to see them. So long as there has been no demonstration of its peculiar effectiveness and a shortage of professionals exists, multiple therapy in which therapists outnumber clients will remain a fascinating, but seldom used, approach. The interests of today mainly are directed, instead, at reducing the investment of time that one therapist has to make in one client, either by increasing the number of persons the therapist sees in a given appointment or by eliminating him from direct contacts with his clients.

Some indirect methods of treatment are not properly regarded as psychotherapy nor do they necessarily yield a saving of professional time. However, they may be the only means to provide assistance. This is often true with infants and children, whose disturbed patterns of behavior may be alleviated by parental counseling or environmental manipulation. For example, a child who appears unhappy and depressed may be responding to a lack of mothering or stimulation (Bowlby, 1951); treatment could be provided by advising his parents to cuddle and to play with him (Kawabata, 1966). This cuddling and stimulation would be therapeutic, perhaps, but it would no more be psychotherapy than the usual mothering that children receive.

The most famous case of indirect psychotherapy was Freud's psychoanalysis of Little Hans (Freud, 1959). This youngster was seen by his father, who would mail reports to Freud, and then receive advice as to how he should proceed and what communications he should direct to his son. However, despite the successful outcome of the analysis, Freud was not especially impressed by the innovative aspects of his treatment and regarded them as the exigencies of handling a very young client.

Today, there is a growing enthusiasm for capitalizing on the strengths of parents and helping them to deal with the problems presented by their children in a corrective manner. Guerney (1964) has reported obtaining very favorable results with what he has termed "filial therapy." He trains parents to use a client-centered method of play therapy with their disturbed children while they are in their homes. Since the parents receive their training in groups, more children receive help than would have if Guerney had attempted to treat each child personally.

Yet parents are not the only persons whose help could be enlisted by the therapist in aiding his clients. Traditionally, psychiatric social workers have called on the client's relatives and friends to assist in his treatment. Outside the circle of the family and close friends, therapists at one time or another have endorsed teachers, clergymen, nurses, attendants, employers, police officers, probation officers, neighbors, fellow patients, and cell mates, not only as valuable resources, but also as often the only means to provide psychotherapy. Given imagination and the use of appropriate safeguards, the list of therapist-surrogates is unlimited.

Indirect psychotherapy does not even require the physical presence of a person other than the client. With the availability of all kinds of marvelous inventions for communication, treatment in a very real and immediate sense can take place over distances of time and space. The most common piece of hardware is the telephone. It is so ubiquitous and, sadly, at times so annoying that its advantages can fail to be appreciated. Yet the telephone does provide meaningful, convenient communications between therapists and clients in emergencies, when meetings are not possible, and in dealing with crises that develop between regularly scheduled appointments.

Saul (1951) described a situation in which the patient's transference took the extreme and peculiar form of being unable to talk in the presence of the analyst. Here the telephone literally came to the rescue, for it made the continuation of the analysis possible until the time that the transference was resolved and in-person sessions could be resumed. However, the saving of professional time in this case was negligible, and beside the point. Similarly, Wittson and his colleagues (1961) reported their use of two-way television to conduct group therapy. Since both the therapist and the group were televised, the only advantage of the television was to enable meetings that might not otherwise have taken place because of distances or disabilities. Of course, this demonstrated the potential for an efficient network of two or more stations that could tie in with a consultant-therapist.

A number of highly ingenious and economical uses of equipment have been reported that attempt to nudge the therapist out of the therapy hour, and these attempts raise questions about the necessity of the intense human relationship that is sometimes thought to be the *sine qua non* of psychotherapy. Efforts to program a computer to respond appropriately to statements of a client (Colby, Watt, and Gilbert, 1966) constitute perhaps the ultimate in sophistication. A less ambitious project required juvenile delinquents simply to talk into a tape recorder (Schwitzgebel, 1963). These adolescents were recruited primarily on the basis of their record of delinquency, were hired to participate in the research, and were "employed" in their neighborhood. They were told that they were free to say whatever they wished during the recording sessions for which they were being paid. At first they just "gabbed," but within a short period many of the delinquents began expressing feelings of anger, worthlessness, and depression; and there was a significant decline in their antisocial activities.

Schwitzgebel did not feel that the tape recorders were crucial to the success of his study. What he believed to have been of most importance was that these youngsters were treated with respect. They were made to feel that their contribution to the research was valuable, and instead of being approached with the idea of having psychotherapy arbitrarily imposed upon them, the investigators asked them for *their* help. Schwitzgebel's conclusion suggests that talking by the client, in and of itself, can be therapeutic, *but that the essence of psychotherapy is communication to the client*.

This same attitude, that a communication of respect and a concern for the welfare of clients is required in psychotherapy, while gadgetry may serve primarily as a means for implementing the attitude, was expressed again by Schwitzgebel (1969) in an article in a popular magazine. After describing a belt that contained a two-way radio, so rigged that a client wearing one could receive a reassuring signal from his therapist who would be some distance away, Schwitzgebel remarked: "That 'someone cares' is perhaps more important than *what* they care about." To be more precise, it is of most importance that someone communicates that he cares.

Often this simple observation about the relative importance of gadgets is lost in the enthusiasm for a new device or medium by which to transmit messages, when these contrivances have no intrinsic merit. It is their function that is significant. The therapist himself can be viewed as but one means of communication, and thus it is conceivable that he can be supplanted by any device that proves to be more effective than he. For example, one task of the therapist is to serve as a mirror, in the sense that he reflects or communicates to the client his ways of behaving. Yet under some circumstances perhaps an actual mirror would accomplish similar results. As shall soon be seen, such a proposal has met with some success when it was more elaborately employed.

Geertsma and Reivich (1965) claimed that a young woman who had the opportunity to see videotapes of her therapy sessions made impressive gains in realistic self-appraisal. Similarly, Cornelison (1966) videotaped the behavior of alcoholics and psychotics while they were on their mental hospital wards, and then had them see how they looked. The impact of watching their own atypical acts apparently led many of them to modify their behavior for the better. Here, unlike the situation that obtained when the delinquents spoke into tape recorders, there was communication to the client, since the therapist selected for viewing those scenes that represented his understanding of how the client behaved abnormally. Cornelison dubbed this technique "Self-Image Experience," and it is a form of psychotherapy that might conceivably be refined to bring about a sizable saving of professional time.

Long before there were videotapes and the Self-Image Experience, the Iroquois Indians told the legend of their hero Deganawidah (*Life* Editors, 1961). He was not a hero of warfare or battle, but a man of courage, similar to the prophets of the Old Testament. His aim was to unite the Indians in a brotherhood of peace, and he traveled among them spreading his message of Righteousness (that there should be justice and honor among men and nations), Health (that the mind and body should be sound, and from this soundness would come reasonableness and peace), and Power (that the people should respect their traditions, laws, and customs).

During his journey, Deganawidah was told of a man who ate the flesh of humans. He wished to see this man in order to reform him and went to the cannibal's home. The home was empty, with signs that its owner was in pursuit of food. Deganawidah decided that it might be best to climb to the roof and wait beside the smoke hole until the man returned.

Soon the man appeared, carrying with him a corpse. As he made ready to prepare his grisly meal, he placed a kettle of water on the fire, and looked upon its surface. There he saw not his own reflection, but the face of Deganawidah, who was peering down on the scene through the smoke hole in the roof. However, the man assumed the reflected face to be his own. This reflection puzzled him, for it was not the face of a cannibal, but that of a man of wisdom and righteousness. His reaction to this bit of cognitive dissonance or to this discrepancy between his Real Self and Ideal Self, as psychologists might say, was to empty the kettle and to be overcome by feelings of guilt. Deganawidah came down to comfort him, to convert him, and eventually to name him, Hiawatha. This story, aside from its charm, suggests that the presentation to the client of scenes of his appropriate behaviors may also have salubrious effects.

Perhaps the ultimate in the thrifty use of professional time, though highly questionable ethically, is an approach described by DiMascio and Brooks (1961). An obsessive-compulsive woman was asked to participate in her analytic sessions while in a room all by herself. She was told to free associate and was informed that her talk was being monitored and her behavior observed by an unseen therapist. Actually, there was no therapist present. Nevertheless, the woman spoke freely and virtually nonstop twice a week for six sessions, at which time the procedure was terminated. The woman believed that she had made significant progress, and the tapes of her verbalizations supported her impression. These recordings indicated not only that she had moved from superficial talk about her work to the production of intimate material about her family, but also disclosed evidences of a transference relationship to her nonexistent analyst. If nothing else, a ruse of this kind demonstrates that the actual presence of a therapist is not essential to the practice of psychotherapy, so long as the therapist has phenomenological reality.

In general, the research that has been considered in this section suggests that indirect forms of psychotherapy are particularly appropriate when the client believes that his problems or symptoms do not require professional assistance, and when the presence of a therapist is severely threatening. Under such circumstances, the lack of face-to-face contacts with a professional therapist is probably not perceived as a rejection or a lapse in professional responsibilities, but as a plan of assistance that is consistent with the client's beliefs. Moreover, when the cooperation of parents or relatives of the client is enlisted as an important part of the treatment endeavor, the counseling or guidance of them can serve to build their self-esteem, rather than constituting a threat or imposition. So too with the reluctant client, who has customarily been regarded as resistant to the work of the therapist, indirect approaches may be best. In fact, since what is direct and what is indirect are relative, the techniques that have been discussed here may be the most straightforward route to assisting certain clients.

VARYING THE NUMBER OF CLIENTS

Among professional therapists there is little question that it is possible to see more than one client at a time in what is known, broadly speaking, as group therapy. This is a fairly recent, and still somewhat suspect, development. Group therapy did not become popular until the 1930s, and it was not widely used until the 1940s (Reisman, 1966). Even then the coincidence of large numbers of World War II veterans in need of treatment and the vigorous emergence of group approaches caused some professionals to view this form of psychotherapy as an illegitimate offspring, sired by expedience and mothered by do-gooders. Since the shortage of therapists is still with us, there is still the attitude that group therapy is a product more of necessity than of desirability, and that it is in many respects inferior to individual treatment. However, this attitude is becoming less widely held, and the value of seeing clients in groups is increasingly appreciated. There are even occasions when group therapy is seen as preferable to individual treatment.

Group therapy has four unique advantages. One, it is less threatening to those clients who would find being alone in a room with a therapist or being required to talk at length very demanding tasks. Two, it enables clients who find it difficult to examine themselves and discuss their problems to derive benefit from hearing others give expression to their feelings, insights, conflicts, and ways of dealing with situations. Three, it is an immediate comfort to some clients to realize that there are others with similar, perhaps worse, problems than their own (Corsini, 1957). Four, it is economical because it allows two or more clients to be seen at one time by a therapist.

However, an equally impressive list of disadvantages can be presented for group therapy. One, for some clients, being seen in a group presents an insurmountable obstacle to discussing problems of an intimate or socially damaging nature. Two, there can be times when the group is so monopolized by a client that no one else has the opportunity to talk. Three, clients who may earnestly desire help may be unable to obtain it through no fault of their own, but because of the disruptive behavior of other members of the group. Four, at times the group members can be excessively hostile to one another and come up with misleading and destructive suggestions, interpretations, and bits of advice.

Of course, it is the task of the therapist to minimize the occurrence of these disadvantages, to turn potentially damaging situations into insightful experiences, and to salvage what he can when things do not work out. Nevertheless, it is best to avoid disasters, rather than to handle them with skill and aplomb, and to that end criteria have been proposed for the judicious selection of group therapy members.

Standards for selection that at first seemed obvious and sensible were based on age, intelligence, severity of disturbance, and sex. The best clients for this approach were thought to be neither too young nor too old, of at least average intellectual functioning, in reasonable contact with reality, and of the same sex for a given group. This seemed to rule out children, the elderly, retardates, psychotics, and some persons who were brain damaged. Yet almost from the moment they were proposed, one therapist or another has taken delight in reporting gratifying results when he has ignored these restrictions. Thus the trend has been to find that selection standards err on the side of prudence, and that presumptive statements quickly die and become ghosts that haunt their authors.

Still, there is a general rule about homogeneity of the group that has held up over time. Although no particular category of clients is excluded, it is argued that the members of a group should be similar in their ability to participate in the treatment. Whitaker and Lieberman (1964) have stated specifically that the vulnerability of the clients should be about the same, that is, a person who cannot tolerate the anxiety he experiences about problems that the rest of the group is eager to discuss should be excluded, as should the person who insists on discussing matters that the rest of the group cannot tolerate. Furthermore, Whitaker and Lieberman believe it is wise to refuse to enroll someone in a group where he would be regarded, not as an individual, but as a stereotype, for example, one or two women in a group where they are far outnumbered by men, a Negro in a white group, an adolescent in a group of adults. If nothing else, these precautions are amenable to experimental test.

Further, there are certain groups of individuals that should be seen as a collective unit. Married couples and families are such groups, as are any variety of groupings in which the members are required to work together in some way. Here group therapy seems particularly appropriate when the members complain of problems in communication, accommodation, and cooperation; as, for example, when a member of the group is scapegoated, and the others bemoan his faults and build themselves up at his expense.

Family therapy has been discussed at some length by Ackerman (1961), and marital counseling has been practiced from time immemorial. An unusual approach to the latter is what Bach (1963) referred to as "fight-training." Couples are helped to evaluate their methods of quarreling and to alter those patterns of hostile behavior so that they become constructive, rather than destructive. This is accomplished by the therapist pointing out what is implied in the communications of the clients and making explicit what impact these messages have. The aim is not to prevent fights, but to assist the couple to express their aggression in an honest and helpful manner, to change their fighting into a therapeutic experience that is of benefit to both parties.

Another form of therapy where the ratio of clients to therapist is two to one is what Finney (1965) calls "partnership therapy." Clients are paired by the therapist on the basis of some relevant criterion, such as problem, education, values, and are seen together. They interact with one another or talk directly with the therapist, and aside from the fact that they may be referred to as "partners," there does not seem to be anything that distinguishes this from group treatment.

It seems safe to say that group therapy approaches will be with us for some time, as will some of the questions that this method generates. Ideally, how many clients should be seen in any one group? Suggestions for group size usually call for six to twelve members, but the matter has certainly not been decided by any body of evidence. Is it more effective to have large lecture or small discussion groups, or perhaps a combination of the two? Whatever the answer, it is clear that therapists do see more than one client at a time, so that the number of clients seen in psychotherapy is not definitive. One more word. Just as there has been a tendency to recommend individual psychotherapy to almost everyone on the supposition that it can do no harm, so there has been a tendency to permit a heterogeneity of clients to enter into group therapy on the supposition that in any case group treatment would do no good. Research indicates that both suppositions are wrong (Bergin, 1966; Rogers, 1967; Pattison, 1965; Gundlach, 1967), and that group therapy can be an effective and efficient method of treatment when it is employed judiciously.

CONTROLS OF THE THERAPIST

The therapy hour is generally, and often romantically, recognized to be a period in which the client can experience considerable freedom. Yet it must also be acknowledged that like every other social situation, the meeting of therapist and client has certain rules, regulations, and conventions. There is general agreement that an appointment is sacrosanct. It should be kept, and it should begin and end at the designated times. If the client breaks an appointment for any flimsy reason, if he breaks them repeatedly for what sound like very good ones, if he comes late, and if he tries, no matter how cleverly, to stay beyond his allotted time, then his therapist is obliged to mention his behavior and to ask the reasons for it.

Therapists generally agree that they would not allow their clients to injure themselves or anyone else. If at all possible, suicides, homicides, and other violently aggressive acts are prevented. Nor is the client permitted to destroy the therapist's property, although he is free to talk about this, or any other act of aggression. These limits or restrictions are so reasonable and so much in keeping with the best interests of all parties concerned that it is hardly conceivable that there would be circumstances that would merit their violation.

The very existence of these basic controls gives meaning to the freedom that the client experiences in psychotherapy. For the client's realization that the therapist will help to keep aggressive inclinations from being put into action enables them to be expressed verbally with some assurance that what is discussed will not be allowed to get out of hand. This assurance is very important, and for some persons is virtually a need that they have to feel certain is filled. For example, it is not uncommon for therapists to have clients who attribute a strength and stamina to them that is sufficient to be overwhelming, even when the reality of the situation is such that the therapist would be hard put to control those clients who sought to act out their impulses. Quite likely it is the power, both intellectual and physical, that clients frequently ascribe to their therapists that is of some significance in helping them to feel safe, hence to speak freely.

Nevertheless, these controls seem to be so just, although ordinarily they do not even have to be made explicit, that many therapists believe their method of treatment allows for an unusual degree of freedom. But freedom to do what? In the end, they refer to the client's being free to say whatever he wishes during the hour. This modest degree of freedom, the freedom of speech, is thought to be unique to psychotherapy, and it is held to be of great significance. Some therapists even argue that the client's experiencing of this freedom provides the impetus for his growth (Rogers, 1961; Boigon, 1965). Yet even in the matter of speech, is the client actually free? The answer is "not really."

Among those who practice psychotherapy, it is usually understood that the client is not really free to talk about whatever he wants. This freedom is qualified by the stipulation that the conversation will turn on matters of some personal importance. The therapist does not expect, nor does he want, the hour to be filled with chitchat, an analysis of current events on the world scene, or a presentation and critique of a theory. Further, it is assumed that the client is aware of this limitation. Therefore if he persists in describing incidents or matters that seem irrelevant, the therapist will wonder why he continues to make use of their time in this way, and will suspect either the working of resistances or inhibitions. Moreover, this suspicion is usually expressed and "taken up," or discussed, with the client. Thus an important task of the therapist is to assess the meaningfulness and relevance of the client's communications, to judge when they are consequential and when they are evasive, and to promote the flow of significant discourse—the implication being that the client is not free to be impersonal in his talk for too long.

This restriction can also be seen at work in the fundamental rule of psychoanalytic treatment, free association: the client is to report whatever comes into his consciousness without subjecting it to critical scrutiny. Here is a situation that seems eminently free. Yet it is not free, both because the analyst assumes the associations are determined and because it is his prerogative, not the client's, to decide when the rule is being followed and when it is not.

Accordingly, despite the relative freedom to speak in the therapy hour, most therapists exercise some control over the client's speech. We are belaboring this point because many therapists overlook it and assume that the quintessence of psychotherapy is freedom, to the extent that they may not appreciate the significance of the few limits that they do impose.

Of course, there are therapists who claim to be impartial about whether or not their clients speak. Although they recognize that verbal communication is a major vehicle for therapeutic exchanges, they do not regard it as essential for constructive changes to take place. They have emphasized time and again that talk, in and of itself, is no index of successful psychotherapy (Rogers, 1942; Powdermaker and Frank, 1953; May et al., 1958), and their clinical impression has been supported by the results of a study conducted by Smith, Bassin, and Froehlich (1960). These investigators found no relationship between degree of verbal participation in group therapy and changes in attitudes toward authority figures. Some of their clients who talked a great deal changed very little, while some who said very little appeared to change a great deal. But despite these findings, most therapists do not accept silences and speech with equal favor.

Virtually all therapists feel more comfortable and certain of what is going on if the client is talking rather than sitting in silence. That is because a silence is intrinsically ambiguous. It can signify that the client is relaxed and peaceful or that he is very frightened, that he is angry or that he is sad, that he is engaging the therapist in a competitive struggle, or that he is groping for the right words with which to express himself. To know what the silence means, the therapist must make some comment about it; and if it persists, he must repeatedly ask for clarification since its meaning can shift.

In addition, most frequently psychotherapy is explicitly structured so that the client understands that his job is to talk. Thus any failure to speak is immediately recognized by both him and the therapist as inappropriate, as a sign of resistance. Psychoanalysis is structured in this way, so that analysts deal very actively with silences to get the client talking again, and talking about subjects that are meaningful. Some idea can be gained about the importance that therapists attach to talk by presenting a few of the techniques that have been developed to promote its occurrence.

Techniques to Promote Client Communication

1. *Offering a Moderate Interpretation or Clarification*

Psychoanalytic therapists will often make an interpretation about the significance of the client's silence, and these interpretations seem to be effective in enabling the resumption of speech (Auld and White, 1959). The interpretations that appear to be of greatest usefulness are not far-fetched and seem to hit the client immediately as "Aha, by George, you've got something there!" Speisman (1959) has suggested that the just right, "good," correct interpretation is moderate in its remoteness from what has gone on, that is, it is neither deep nor superficial.

Moderation appears to promote the therapeutic process in client verbalizations. Parker (1967) found that therapists who tended to dominate their clients and to respond to them in a directive manner were less successful than those who did not in bringing about client statements indicative of understanding and insight. Similarly, Frank and Sweetland (1962) noted that in the verbal interaction in treatment, direct questioning by the therapist elicited answers from the client that elaborated the problems, but that seldom led to insight or statements indicative of understanding. However, when the therapist clarified feelings or offered interpretations, the client was likely to respond with remarks of comprehension and self-awareness. These findings support the view that an authoritative, inquisitorial approach tends to stifle client spontaneity, and that it is less successful than a moderate, integrative approach in furthering the client's attempts to understand himself.

Although we must recognize that "moderate" is a relative term, Truax and Carkhuff's (1964) clarification of what they mean by "accurate empathy" seems to provide a basis for making reliable judgments: ". . . responding to client affect just below the surface and labeling, identifying, or emphasizing it . . . *not* making connections between past and present or being diagnostic or theoretical." Since making connections between past and present is one of the major tasks of the analyst (Menninger, 1958), and since the studies we have just considered suggest that such interpretations are appropriate in psychotherapy, that particular negative injunction by Truax and Carkhuff appears to be more a function of their therapeutic orientation than a necessary and essential stipulation. At any rate, "moderate" is a term that is not specific, that represents a range bordered by the obvious and the obtuse, and that when applied to an interpretation or clarification describes a remark that can stimulate the client's speech.

2. *Providing a Stimulus for Discussion*

Widroe and Davidson (1961) asked their patients to write accounts of their daily activities, and then to discuss these accounts in the treatment hour. They found that when something was written down, it served not only as a useful starting point for discussion, but it also had the added advantage of being a permanent record that could be referred to when needed.

Kluge and Thren (1951) encouraged their patients to lie down and to wait passively for any mental image that might appear to them. This would last for approximately 25 minutes, and during that period all the images were supposed to be reported. Afterwards, the patient's productions would be discussed and interpreted in much the same way that a Rorschach test protocol is analyzed—which reminds us that some therapists make use of testing and test material as a spur to conversation.

The "associative anamnesis" is a device developed by Deutsch (1960). A loud sound occurs at the beginning of the interview, and this is supposed to trigger important pre-verbal, childhood concerns. The client's associations to the sound provide clues to these early problems. The imagination is boggled by the host of stimuli—crashing cymbals,, flashing lights, blasts of perfume—that could be evaluated for their effectiveness in arousing the recall of early conflicts.

Levinson (1965) found it helpful to have pets in his office. They served not only as a topic of conversation, but also as warm, furry objects to which the clients could relate. Also pets can provide a "homey" touch, and perhaps make it easier for some clients to feel at ease.

The "behind your back technique" (Corsini, 1953) is used at times in group therapy. The procedure has a client sit with his back to the group or remain hidden behind a screen while the other members discuss his personality characteristics and behavior. When they are finished he returns to the group and reacts to what has been said about him.

Reactions of the client are also solicited to the dramatization of his conflicts as if he were on trial in a court of law, a technique called "psychotrial" (Medina, 1965); and to a videotape of a play that depicts a problem situation, tape-a-drama (Catanzaro, 1967).

Finally, to indicate that this list is not exhaustive, we note that in an article Zerka Moreno (1959) commented on but 20 out of approximately 300 techniques peculiar to psychodrama, for example, hallucinatory psychodrama, double technique, multiple double technique, and mirror technique.

3. *Reducing Inhibitions to Speech*

The use of drugs and hypnosis in this connection has a long history. In the days before LSD achieved its outstanding and unfortunate notoriety, Hein (1963) reported that it was helpful in overcoming resistances and enabling patients to talk of unconscious material, particularly in cases of character neurosis, compulsions, perversions, chronic anxieties, and sociopathic behaviors. Evidently there are times when inhibitions are reduced by bringing the client to a state of LSD intoxication by administering a dose of 100 micrograms of the drug (Hausner and Dolezal, 1966); the effectiveness of this method can be gauged roughly by the observation of a random sample of cocktail parties.

Sherman (1961) has suggested to the analyst that he appear to go along with the client's negative attitudes, for example, if the person is silent, to act as though this is what you want him to be. It is hoped that this bit of negative psychology will get the client to disengage himself from a struggle with the therapist and enable him to talk.

In general, those things that are commonly known to reduce inhibitions have been suggested and tried at one time or another in psychotherapy. Accordingly, it is not too surprising, though admittedly it arouses mixed feelings, to have nudity advocated as a promising means for the stimulation of, *inter alia,* conversation (Lawrence, 1969).

4. *Conditioning Speech*

The therapist may intentionally stimulate the flow of speech or the discussion of certain topics by his verbal and nonverbal expressions of interest, approval, and concern. It is even possible that he may reinforce his client in ways that are so subtle that he is not aware of his making use of them. Whether they do this deliberately or not, apparently many therapists condition their clients, and the option available to them is how systematically they wish to go about it. For some therapists this presents a problem because they make every effort to avoid influencing the choices of their clients. Certainly the Rogerian approach to psychotherapy emphasizes the creation of conditions in which the person feels free; if anything, it has been criticized for its too serious attempt to prevent any intrusion of the therapist's values into the hour. Yet an analysis of tape recordings of interviews conducted by Carl Rogers (Truax, 1966) demonstrates an unintentional use of verbal conditioning by him, and fully supports Krasner's

(1962) contention that the therapist may be regarded as a more or less effective social reinforcement machine.

The most direct attack on stimulating speech is to give rewards for its occurrence, and this could be combined with a method suggested by Heckel, Wiggins, and Salzberg (1962), who conditioned their clients to talk by presenting an unpleasant auditory stimulus whenever they were silent.

A note of caution in this area is that what is rewarding or aversive must be determined for the individual. For example, Miller (1964) has criticized note taking, a common practice in psychoanalysis, for its negative effects. He sees it as an aversive stimulus, creating distance between the therapist and the client and interfering with communication. However, it is equally possible to observe note taking serving the function of a reward. A client will attend to those subjects that the therapist deems worthwhile, as evidenced by his writing down the content with zest, and may even be solicitous about the accurate recording of data, while pacing the tempo to insure that no precious detail is lost. What is an effective reinforcer must be determined for each individual.

These techniques of the therapist indicate the importance of communication to him and the importance of communication in psychotherapy. They suggest that communication, in one way or another, is something that all therapists do. But what does he communicate to his clients? In the techniques we have already presented, there is a sketchy answer, and perhaps this can be delineated more boldly by examining some of the techniques employed to modify symptoms.

Techniques to Alter Symptoms

When a person goes to a therapist for help, he presents a statement of his problem. Those things that bother him and those aspects of his behavior that deeply trouble others comprise his pattern of symptoms. He is very much interested in having these symptoms eliminated or reduced in severity, and he expects the therapist, by virtue of his role in society, his education, his certificates, and his fee, to be of assistance to him. But the therapist, depending on his particular orientation, may not agree with the client's concept of how he can best be of service.

At the very least, many therapists are going to be disappointing to the client because they do not make the symptoms go away immediately. Moreover, their attitude toward the symptom is likely to differ from the client's. Psychoanalytic theory, which in its basic formulations is very widely accepted, views symptoms as often, but not always, a compromise expression of a wish or impulse and a repressive or inhibiting force. There is an unconscious conflict that is represented by the symptom, and it is that conflict that must be treated. The symptom itself is relatively unimportant, and it is expected that there will no longer be any need for its existence when the conflict is resolved. Thus the therapist's first step may be to point out to his client that the very thing that motivated him to seek help is actually of little significance.

Frequently another surprise awaits the client. He has sought out professional aid because he does not feel able to deal with his problems, and yet he will now be told that much of the work involved in solving his difficulties will be his own. Frank (1961, p. 98) correctly stated: "All methods of promoting healing or attitude change through personal influence seem to require the object of the influence to participate actively in the proceedings." However, there are differences among therapists in how much responsibility or control they are willing to delegate or assume.

Some therapists, such as behavior therapists, consider the client's expectations about the immediate relief or treatment of his symptoms as a reasonable objective. They regard the symptom as a bit of behavior that can be modified or shaped as any other bit of behavior, and they see themselves as experts in techniques that can accomplish such modifications. These therapists assume considerable responsibility and control, and in a very obvious way they play an active, directive role in treating the symptoms. However, many other therapists believe, as has already been noted, that the client's attitudes about his symptoms are incorrect, and that before anything else can be accomplished these attitudes must be modified.

In psychoanalysis the opening therapeutic strategy is to minimize the client's concern about the absence of a frontal assault aimed toward the alleviation of his symptom and to focus his attention on the identification of underlying conflicts. It is recognized that two major approaches can be employed to relieve the symptoms. The first method is definitely not favored by analysts, and it works by increasing the inhibiting forces, even though this may eventually have undesirable repercussions: "By a 'repression of symptoms' (techniques that increase the patient's anxiety or fear of punishment and thereby the force of his repressions) the pressure of the repressed will necessarily be increased and sooner or later new symptoms will be formed" (Fenichel, 1945). The other method, and the one invariably employed in psychoanalysis, is to seek to reduce the client's anxiety to an optimum level, one that will continue to motivate him toward self-understanding, yet enable him to recognize his conflicts, and allow the expression of his impulses in a socially acceptable fashion.

Rogerian therapy, individual psychology, existential analysis, and a number of other forms of psychotherapy frequently see the client striving to divest himself of the responsibility for his change. The symptoms may be virtually unloaded on the therapist by the client, who then sits back and waits passively for something to be done about them. Accordingly, these therapists regard as their initial task to get the client to recognize that much of the work to be done in bringing about change will be his own. Their treatment strategy is usually to reduce anxiety to a level that will allow the person to feel free to make choices and to assume responsibility.

These differences among therapists in beliefs about symptoms, hence treatment goals, can make for significant differences in how they practice psychotherapy. For their clients, particularly those who are able to exercise choice in the therapy they receive, this can translate into marked differences in how much time, money, and of themselves they will have to invest. One would suppose that professional ethics would demand that a statement be made to the client informing him of the existence of these differences and of the therapist's convictions, thus enabling him to make an informed decision as to the psychotherapy he receives. Yet this is not the practice.

Of course, whatever the form of psychotherapy received, all therapists agree that ultimately it is important to help the client with his symptoms. He has come to the therapist feeling unable to change his own behavior and emotions. He believes that he has tried everything, although upon reflection it becomes clear that he has actually tried nothing, and now feeling defeated he recognizes the need for help. His therapist may take charge, congratulate him on his wisdom in seeking professional counsel, radiate optimism, and give, especially to clients who are somewhat dependent, a feeling of hope and relief. Or his therapist may sit back in his chair, as Alfred Adler often used to do, fold his hands, say nothing, and perhaps give his client a feeling of perplexity and the impetus to reconsider his motivation and intentions. Yet under both of these very different sets of circumstances the therapist, by his calm and assured manner, indicates that the symptoms need not be alarming, that there is a chance of change for the better, and that the problem is not an unfamiliar one.

In addition to respect and a wish to be of help, all therapists communicate an understanding of the client's problems. The understanding may be expressed in the form of statements describing what needs to be done to modify the symptoms, it may be conveyed in attempts to capture the implicit meanings and feelings of the client's messages, or it may be transmitted by an attitude of composure and confidence and a calm, "I see." All forms of this communication of understanding of the person should be regarded as psychotherapy. Tentatively, the communication of person-related understanding, respect, and a wish to be of help defines psychotherapy. Let us now see how such a definition is useful in deciding which techniques employed by therapists are part of psychotherapy and which are not.

1. *Modifying the Client's Attitudes about His Symptoms*

In Morita therapy (Kora and Sato, 1958) the aim is to have the client realize that his suffering is not unique or abnormal, but instead that it is an almost universal fact of the human condition. (We may recall that one of the advantages attributed to group therapy is that it enables the person to see immediately that he is not alone in having troubles.) Rather than feeling that the existence of problems is exceptional, the client is encouraged to view difficulties and unhappiness as part of life, and to regard any hope for his years to be without fear, sadness, and worry as futile. What he must do is to resign himself to what is inevitable and to strive for a feeling of satisfaction and contentment with what he has. In this way the client is urged to accept himself for what he is, to live at peace with his symptoms, and to make the best accommodation to his world that he can. Yet, clearly, in this very process of becoming reconciled to no change, there is involved change, which at the very least would reduce the client's feelings of anxiety and depression.

Frankl (1960) has developed a technique that he refers to as "paradoxical intention." Following the client's description of his symptoms, he is urged to "manufacture" or to display them as much as he likes or at will. Supposedly, since he cannot produce them with the same vigor and complex of feelings, his attitude toward them changes from a fear and embarrassment about their appearance to one of amusement and a kind of fondness for them. As he becomes able to stand aside and laugh and joke about his symptoms, the client also feels able to assume responsibility for their occurrence. Gerz (1966) has reported that of 51 phobic and obsessive-compulsive patients treated largely by means of paradoxical intention, about 88% recovered or showed considerable improvement, which certainly commends the technique for further study. It is alleged that the principle on which paradoxical intention operates is that a person cannot voluntarily produce an involuntary response; cf. negative practice (Dunlap, 1932).

In what is called by Corey (1966) "reverse format," the client is told that he does not need to change, and that he should accept himself the way he is. Of course the hope is that the client will change by no longer feeling the need for change, as in Morita therapy, and we may note that in each of these techniques the aim is to enable the person to take his symptoms less seriously, that is, the therapist communicates that he understands, and there is really not that much to worry about.

2. *Reducing Negative Feelings*

The negative feelings are those that people ordinarily find unpleasant, such as fear, hostility, and sadness. Direct attacks on these emotions have made use of drugs, the implantation of radioactive Yttrium 90 seeds into the substantia innominata of depressed patients (Knight, 1965), electroshock, psychosurgery, self-stimulation by means of electrodes inserted in the septal area of the limbic system (Heath, 1964), and relaxing in a pool of water (Crumbaugh, Salzberg, and Agee, 1966). These techniques are mentioned merely to suggest that psychotherapeutic approaches are not alone in this area.

Almost all psychotherapists assist clients to express feelings by verbal communication. The hope is that the release of emotions will reduce their intensity, or the tension experienced by the person when he seeks to put how he feels into action. This technique, catharsis in a broad sense, is used widely. The therapist tries to acknowledge the feelings of the client, to label them, and to help the person to become aware of them. Kidd and Walton (1966) described a variation of this technique that they employed with ten aggressive boys. These youngsters were encouraged to throw darts at photographs of persons toward whom they had expressed hostility. The result was that there was a significant reduction in the boys' acts of overt aggression toward people who were not members of their families, although there was no such effect for family members (perhaps because family members continued to be sources of frustration). However, despite the therapeutic effectiveness of the technique, it is not psychotherapy. Nor by the definition is any expression of feeling or activity of the client to be regarded as psychotherapy, since psychotherapy is an activity of the "therapist."

Conditioning therapies attempt to reduce fear or anxiety by deconditioning, reciprocal inhibition, and systematic desensitization (Wolpe, 1958; Eysenck and Rachman, 1965; Wolpe and Lazarus, 1966; Ulmann and Krasner, 1969). Essentially, the therapist helps the client to feel relaxed under circumstances where earlier he would have felt frightened, that is, relaxational responses are elicited and paired with what were anxiety-arousing stimuli, thus diminishing their arousal value for negative affect.

A very different technique, implosive therapy (Stampfl and Levis, 1967), tries to make the person feel as anxious as possible to the fear-arousing cues, but in a setting where the rewards for feeling that way are considerably diminished. Underlying both techniques, implosion and reciprocal inhibition, seem to be the principles that (a) the therapist fully understands how to alleviate the symptoms, and (b) that you cannot feel two ways about the same thing at exactly the same time (if you feel somewhat relaxed and in control of your emotions, you do not feel uncontrollable fear). Whatever the explanation for the effectiveness of these techniques, they do seem to be effective (DeLeon and Mandell, 1966; Hogan and Kirchner, 1967; Levis and Carrera, 1967). But to what extent they are psychotherapy would depend on an evaluation of the communications of the therapists who employ conditioning.

3.   Increasing Negative Feelings

When an aim of treatment is to assist the person to avoid thinking about or doing something, the therapist may try to achieve this objective by intensifying the unpleasant feelings associated with the act or thought. He may point out the undesirable consequences of persisting in the behavior; he may show the client how he looks, for example, Self-Image Experience; he may express his own negative feelings for the activity, for example, being "genuine" in the relationship; and he may solicit the sanctions of other clients if the person is being seen in some sort of group.

Conditioned inhibition is a procedure that tries to diminish the frequency of a response by having the client practice it and practice it and practice it. At long last, cues of fatigue become associated with the response, and the likelihood that it will be elicited is lowered. This technique has been used to eliminate tics and stuttering, and it is primarily conditioning, not psychotherapy, since it is not predicated on communication by the therapist.

A more direct approach is to pair an unpleasant stimulus with the undesirable response or unfortunately attractive stimulus. For example, administering a painful electric shock when the client smokes or drinks or hiccups. If the therapist punishes the client for imagining the undesirable stimulus, as when he is trying to create an avoidance reaction for something he cannot ask the person to perform (acts of homosexuality, delinquency, etc.), the technique is called "covert sensitization" (Cautela, 1967). This also is not primarily psychotherapy, but conditioning.

4.   Training Appropriate Behavior

There are many techniques that work by encouraging the person to perform certain desirable behaviors and then rewarding him for doing so. Social rewards (smiles, praise, expressions of approval), tokens that can be exchanged for various commodities and privileges, and pieces of food are commonly used reinforcers. The social rewards are regarded as the least demeaning, although it is doubtful that too many people would be wholly satisfied if it were their only remuneration for gainful employment.

Playing a role that one wishes to perform in an actual situation is one technique for developing competence. It is similar in the way it operates to the play of children, which as we know can contribute to the acquisition of social skills and a feeling of mastery. Behavior rehearsal (Gittelman, 1965) is one form of this method. In it the client is asked to enact appropriate responses to situations that arouse negative effects or that he has handled ineptly in the past. His practice in dealing with these situations not only makes them more tolerable, but also allows him to consider acceptable alternatives to his previous patterns of behavior. An important feature of the technique is that the person is presented with a graded series of interpersonal problems, and proceeds from the least to the most distressing. Lazarus (1966) reported that this procedure was significantly more effective than direct advice or Rogerian therapy in improving social skills. While Johnson (1965), who did a follow-up study of psychiatric patients who did and did not receive human relations training, found that the trained group had significantly more men employed and significantly fewer physical complaints than the untrained group ten months after their release from the hospital.

Role reversal is a technique that asks the client to play the role of the object of his feelings, for example, the person toward whom he feels aggressive. Its aim is to promote the client's empathic ability, that is, his understanding of how the other person feels. Ablesser (1962) found the procedure useful in working with juvenile delinquents who were accused of auto theft, and who seemed chastened when they imagined their reactions if someone were to steal their cars.

Some approaches put the client in real life situations such as dancing (Chace, 1953) and camping (Weisman, Mann, and Barker, 1966); or stimulate feelings and awareness of one's own body by tickling (Paige, McNamara, and Fisch, 1964); sensory saturation, a mild "high" induced by touching, smelling, hearing, seeing, and tasting liked objects (Bindrim, 1970); and inducing gagging (Regardie, 1952). Although these and kindred techniques may have a beneficial effect, that is, they may be psychotherapeutic, they are not psychotherapy per se, since, again, they are not predicated upon communication by the "therapist" to the client.

Brayfield (1968) has presented five major methods for the shaping of human behavior, which are relevant to this discussion since all are psychotherapeutic but not all are psychotherapy:

1. The differential reinforcement of responses, particularly giving immediate rewards for the desired behavior. This could be part of psychotherapy.

2. Modeling, or presenting a person who exhibits appropriate behavior, for example, the therapist, for someone else, the client, to emulate. This is definitely not psychotherapy.

3. Expectations, or conveying the belief that improvement and standards of excellence are attainable. This could be part of psychotherapy.

4. Beliefs, or discussing dynamic concepts, thus leading the person to feel he follows that pattern of action associated with the label. This is definitely psychotherapy.

5. Problem solving or decision making, which enables the client to feel personally involved, hence more satisfied with the solution reached, than he would otherwise have been. This could be part of psychotherapy.

What has determined the classification of one method as part of psychotherapy and another as not? Perhaps this can be best explained by hastening to a consideration of the conclusions that have evolved from this chapter.

CONCLUSIONS

This survey of the manipulations of the participants in psychotherapy, despite its brevity, illustrates the remarkable diversity to be found in this method of treatment and leads to the following conclusions. Neither the number of clients nor the presence of a therapist defines psychotherapy, which lends additional support to the contention that the existence of some kind of relationship is not definitive. Further, psychotherapy does not require extraordinary freedom for its practice. What it does require, aside from a client, is a means for communicating with that client. Getting a message across is involved in every method of psychotherapy that has been considered, and in all other forms of psychotherapy that have not been mentioned specifically.

But what makes one form of communication psychotherapy, in contrast to other forms of communication that are not psychotherapy? Is there anything shared by all the different techniques and methods? An analysis of what has been presented suggests three common elements in communications that appear to be psychotherapy: one, there is a wish to be of help to the client; two, in each, respect for the client is implied; and three, in each there is communication of understanding of what the client has said or done, or of what the client might do to improve his condition or behavior. It is the presence of these three elements that distinguishes psychotherapy from other forms of communication. Tentatively, the communication of person-related understanding, respect, and a wish to be of help defines psychotherapy.

CHAPTER 4

An Examination of the Good Therapist Concept

If there is anything that the whole idea of liberalism contradicts, it is the notion of competitive indoctrination. I believe that if we really want human brotherhood to spread and increase until it makes life safe and sane, we must also be certain that there is no one true path by which it may spread.

But it is not easy to banish the notion that there can be universal brotherhood just as soon as everybody gives up his faith and accepts ours. That day may never come, for the richness of human diversity cannot be abolished any more than Mars or Jupiter. Difference is the nature of life, it is part of our moral Universe. Without difference, life would become lifeless. So I reject the idea of conformity, compulsory or complacent, the faith that is swallowed like pills, whole and at once, with no questions asked.

Adlai E. Stevenson

The medium most closely associated with the communication of person-related understanding, respect, and a wish to be of help is that highly trained human being known as the therapist. It is he who has acquired a body of knowledge and a mastery of techniques that he expects will be of assistance to his clients. In his work he makes use of a precious commodity that he has painstakingly earned, an informed judgment.

In this chapter attention will be directed to the therapist's personality characteristics. The discussion will attempt to provide answers to the following questions:

1. Are there certain personality characteristics, aside from those that can reasonably be expected of successful college graduates, that can be said to be peculiar to the good psychotherapist?

2. Are there any qualities specific to the therapist that should be included in the definition of psychotherapy that has been proposed?

THE GOOD CLIENT

Psychotherapy, as professionals tend to conceive of it today, rejects no particular category of people as clients. Its clients are persons of all ages, the impoverished and the wealthy, the intellectually superior and the subnormal, those in robust physical health and those dying (Norton, 1963). To a large extent this state of affairs is a function of the definition of psychotherapy under which many therapists have labored, that is, that psychotherapy is some beneficial process promoted by psychological measures; in other words, that psychotherapy is something that is psychotherapeutic. Under these circumstances it would be difficult, indeed, to argue that any group should be deprived of this helpful method, and at the same time it would be difficult to consider the method's limitations. Quite the contrary. The emphasis, when confronted with failures in treatment, would be turned on the therapist and his techniques. The search would be for adjustments and mistakes in his practice and for personal deficiencies, rather than for certain groups of people who might not be appropriate for psychotherapy as a method of treatment. This was not always the case.

At the beginning of the twentieth century, when the interest in psychotherapy was growing rapidly and the field was new and strange and fragile, there was a different attitude about the usefulness of this form of treatment. Practitioners were few, skepticism was high, even impressions about its effectiveness were meagre. Under those circumstances, the methods had to seem more rigid and less subject to alteration than they do today, if for no other reason than that they be easily taught, understood, and accepted as scientific enterprises. In order to enhance their chances and to present a fitting attitude of caution, psychotherapeutic approaches were originally prescribed for a relatively narrow range of disorders and clientele. Since qualifications appear to be the handmaidens of empirical favor and respectability, attention was given to describing the suitable candidate for psychotherapy.

Freud was among those who were most specific about formulating criteria for the use of psychoanalysis. He saw his method as the treatment par excellence for hysteria and obsessional neurosis, but for other disorders he had less enthusiasm than his followers. Specifically, he believed it to be unsuitable for the treatment of dementia praecox or schizophrenia. Further, he thought that persons beyond a certain age, the elderly, lacked the psychological resilience to be able to profit from it, while he doubted that those who were below average intelligence could be greatly helped.

In addition, Freud was keenly aware of the extensive investment made by analysts in their professional training and in each client that they saw. His concern was that priorities be established so that the best use could be made of the analyst's limited time: ". . . since it (psychoanalysis) necessitates the devotion of long and intense attention to the individual patient, it would be uneconomical to squander such expenditure upon completely worthless persons who happen to be neurotic" (Freud, 1959, originally 1922).

These restrictions were not an idiosyncracy of Freud, nor were they specific to psychoanalysis. Although Adler placed no limits on who might benefit from his method of therapy, individual psychology, he took care to point out that all the clients he had treated had been of at least average intelligence. And in 1942 Carl Rogers, in introducing nondirective therapy, laid down a long list of criteria for the selection of clients best suited to his approach: of at least dull normal intelligence, between the ages of ten and sixty, free of organic impairment and gross instability, able to keep appointments and to cope with life, somewhat autonomous and expressive of feelings, and experiencing tension and a desire to be helped (Rogers, 1942).

However, every limitation connotes a temptation, and no sooner were the boundaries of psychotherapy drawn than tests were made of their inviolability. Thus we find Freud in the 1920s acknowledging that his followers were making efforts to employ psychoanalysis in the treatment of "gross organic diseases." The encouraging reports that accompanied the daring applications of the method softened Freud's position and led him to suppose that with suitable modifications analysis might be extended to a greater number of clients than he had thought.

Perhaps all too quickly the qualifications about the characteristics of the suitable client for psychotherapy were punctured and collapsed. By the 1930s there was general enthusiasm for treating psychotics with psychotherapy; by the 1940s the treatment of "higher-grade" mental defectives was both being advocated and well received (Sarason, 1949). Moreover, along with the zealous application of therapeutic approaches to the entire spectrum of psychiatric disorders came a greatly broadened concept of what constituted disturbed behavior.

Character disorders and the entire range of antisocial activities extended the compass of mental illness to include individuals who did not exhibit symptoms in the usual sense and who felt no desire for personal change. Although it was generally recognized that those clients who were most likely to benefit from psychotherapy were those who were relatively well adjusted and eager to receive the treatment (Stieper and Wiener, 1965), neither the absence of behaviors thought by the person to be in need of change nor his antagonism to the offer of services was sufficient to discourage some psychotherapists from making the effort to provide professional assistance. They argued that under some circumstances a lack of obvious pathology was not as relevant as a request for treatment. In other situations they contended that a client's indifference or active opposition to therapy was no deterrent, but a challenge to devise ways to overcome the resistances and to promote adaptive functioning. Therefore the good client, the one who at least had symptoms and wanted to be helped, was joined by reluctant clients who did not believe they had symptoms and who did not feel a need for help; and the attitude among professionals shifted from a modest, certainly premature, set of guidelines for the selection of clients to, at worst, unabashed declarations of omnipotence and, at best, a mild optimism coupled with a determination to subject what was being done to scientific study.

The consequences of this attitude or assumption that psychotherapy can benefit every psychological disturbance have been totally unnecessary and perhaps even damaging. Needlessly, it has obstructed serious consideration of clients or disorders for which this method of treatment is inefficient or ineffective. Instead, it has led professionals to stress, not the deficiencies and strengths of psychotherapy, but the deficiencies and strengths of psychotherapists. However, this emphasis has not been without its blessings.

Since there was to be practically no selection among clients, the therapist himself became more of an object of study than he might have been otherwise. In point of fact, the therapist had been rather neglected and a number of highly important questions as to his training, personality characteristics, and indispensability begged to be answered. What shall be considered in both this chapter and the next is the value of this examination of the therapist and its relevance for the definition of psychotherapy.

CHARACTERISTICS OF THE GOOD THERAPIST

The question of what personality characteristics go into the making of a good psychotherapist is a fairly straightforward one, and many of the members of the profession have answered it in a fairly straightforward manner. Yet it derives from the assumption that since all methods of psychotherapy have their share of success, most therapists, regardless of their specific practices, must have a highly important something in common. Proceeding from that assumption, it follows that an attempt should be made to identify what that something is, with the thought that by so doing what makes psychotherapy work can be discovered.

There is agreement among all therapists that an understanding of people and a sensitivity to their feelings and communications are essential. It is taken for granted that the practitioners are of at least average intelligence and capable of mastering a given theory and sensibly implementing its techniques, a not unreasonable expectation since few systems of psychotherapy are taught to anyone who has less than a college education. Accordingly, the importance of understanding is stressed by virtually every method of psychotherapy (Ford and Urban, 1963).

Although all therapists should be understanding, the outstanding men and women in the field are often singled out for praise because they are especially so. For example, Paul Federn and August Aichhorn, two eminent psychoanalysts, are described as having brought to their treatment a combination of diagnostic skill, therapeutic zeal, kindness and strength, as well as a detachment that enabled them to understand their patients clearly and without sentimentality (Federn, 1962). Presumably other good therapists embody the same characteristics, and those who would aspire to be good therapists should cultivate those qualities.

An empirical foundation for the belief in the good therapist was the interpretation given to the results of two widely cited studies by Fiedler. The first (Fiedler, 1950a) investigated the meaning of the concept of an "ideal therapeutic relationship" among therapists who differed considerably in their treatment approaches. Yet despite their differences they agreed in their descriptions of the "ideal therapeutic relationship"; empathic, with excellent rapport, and with a therapist who is understanding. This suggested that all therapists strive to develop the same kind of relationship with their clients.

A second study followed soon thereafter (Fiedler, 1950b). This time Fiedler asked three judges to evaluate the taped treatment sessions of therapists of different orientations and to describe the relationships that had been produced. The judgments pointed to the same kind of relationship in the diverse therapies, one characterized by empathy, genuineness, the maintenance of rapport, and a degree of professional detachment. Drawing upon the findings of his research, Fiedler concluded, "relationship *is* therapy" (Fiedler, 1950b).

Fiedler's conclusion was very warmly received by a large number of therapists. Equally well received was his incidental finding that experienced therapists of different positions agreed with each other more in their descriptions than they did with inexperienced therapists of their own position. The implications of these results were both heartening and comforting. They suggested that seasoned therapists, admittedly all men of good will, grow to forget the petty differences that once separated them and become alike in their goals. Here was hope for amicable relationships and a basis for cooperation among the elder statesmen of the profession.

Perhaps the wish to see all therapists, in the end, united in their objectives and methods has been too appealing. Certainly it has resulted in the hasty acceptance of the implications of Fiedler's studies without proper attention paid to the limitations of his research. His findings have been generalized to all therapists, to men and women working in all systems of psychotherapy. Yet just how representative of the population of psychotherapists were his samples? In his first study Fiedler (1950a) had a total of eight therapists: four analysts, two Rogerians, and two eclectics. In his second study Fiedler (1950b) had tapes representing the work of ten therapists: four analysts, four Rogerians, and two Adlerians. At the very least, his sample sizes are not too impressive for any system of psychotherapy, and therapists of many methods were not included. We can also say that because he used Q sorts (descriptive statements supplied by the investigator to the judges who rated them according to how well they applied to the relationship) the research was biased to the finding of agreement in the area to be described, while the relevance of other possible common factors was ignored, for example, the client's recognition of his need for help and change.

Despite their shortcomings, these two studies of Fiedler have had considerable influence. They have been mentioned favorably by Rogers (1951), who has found them congenial with his own hypotheses and beliefs: ". . . therapy has to do with the *relationship,* and has relatively little to do with techniques or with theory and ideology" (Rogers, 1962). And they have had an influence on the interpretation given by investigators to their equivocal findings.

For example, Shostrom and Riley (1968) asked 16 judges in Australia and 24 judges in California to view a film of Carl Rogers, Frederick Perls (Gestalt therapy), and Albert Ellis (rational-emotive therapy) conducting an interview with the same female client. They were to rate these therapists on a number of characteristics: caring, ego-strengthening, encountering, feeling, interpersonal analyzing, reinforcing, self-disclosing, value reorienting, reexperiencing, and pattern analysis (the therapist helps the client to perceive his maladaptive patterns of functioning and to develop better ones). Although the therapists were rated differently on these characteristics, they were judged to exhibit each of them to some extent, a finding that appears to be quite ambiguous. However, the conclusion of the authors was definitely on the side of no differences among therapists: ". . . every therapist may be described as an 'emerging eclectic.' "

Probably no one has been more specific than Carl Rogers about what makes a good therapist. He and his colleagues have at one time or another mentioned five factors: accurate empathy, unconditional positive regard, self-disclosure, concreteness, and genuineness. But it is the last characteristic, genuineness, the notion that within broad and still unspecified limits the words and actions of the therapist should correspond with his own feelings, that has come to seem to Rogers to be of greatest significance: ". . . the person who is able openly to be himself at that moment, as he is at the deepest levels he is able to be, is the effective therapist. Perhaps nothing else is of any importance" (Rogers, 1962).

Rogers' assertion is that psychotherapy is, above all, a positive human relationship, and that the therapist's being himself contributes toward the formation of a meaningful and constructive encounter. Steinzer (1967) expressed a similar point of view in this way: ". . . psychotherapy succeeds according to the ability of the doctor and patient to share in genuine partnership the suffering, joys, changes, and crises that mark the patient's efforts to find meaning and love."

In support of his contention, Rogers (1961) noted a study by G. Halkides in which ratings of genuineness on the part of the therapist were significantly associated with successful outcome of the case. Further research by Truax et al. (1966) provided additional evidence in favor of Rogers' formulations. Although Truax did not use the term "unconditional positive regard," his concept of "nonpossessive warmth" is, for all practical purposes, identical with it. The study itself involved four resident psychiatrists who were randomly assigned 40 patients for a brief period (four months) of psychotherapy. Those therapists who were evaluated as providing high therapeutic conditions (they were judged to be high in accurate empathy, genuineness, and warmth) had 90% of their patients "improve." But the therapists who were judged to offer less empathy, genuineness, and warmth had only 50% of their patients improve. These percentages are certainly dramatically different, even if the actual difference between the two groups, 8 patients, is less impressive, and the contrived nature of the study gives one pause.

Another piece of research in the same vein is that of Lorr (1965). A group of 523 Veterans Administration psychiatric patients evaluated their therapists in terms of 65 statements. A factor analysis of the statements yielded five clusters of therapist characteristics: A (understanding); B (accepting); C (authoritarian); D (independence-encouraging); and E (critical-hostile). When the factors were correlated with ratings of patient improvement, only factors A (understanding) and B (accepting) related significantly, although it must be added not very impressively (+.34 and +.24).

Nevertheless, the consistency of the findings has been impressive. While it has been pointed out that "the type of 'sensitivity' desired—communicated empathy—is possibly not something that even the most empathic or sensitive of us can figure out without being taught" (Linden and Stollak, 1969), the emphasis has been on "natural" human qualities. One study after another has led to the conclusion that therapeutic progress varies as a function of the therapist's warmth (Nash et al., 1957; Feifel and Eells, 1963), expressions of warmth being one aspect of genuineness. This research also has contended that while the good therapist, one who is rated high on genuineness, unconditional positive regard, and accurate empathy, is of help to his clients, the therapist rated low on these characteristics may not only be ineffective, but harmful to his clients (Bergin, 1966). Essentially, since these therapeutically facilitative qualities are highly intercorrelated (Muehlberg, Pierce, and Drasgow, 1969), the good therapist emerges as a person who is friendly and understanding. The ineffective therapist is one who appears to be less friendly, not so understanding, and reserved.

Surprisingly, or perhaps not so surprisingly to those therapists who feel at times that their clients do not appreciate them, the good therapist's virtues often seem to be lost on the people he helps, a finding that caused Hansen, Moore, and Carkhuff (1968) to wonder: "There may, then, be reason to question the client's ability to assess who and what is best for him. Indeed, it is quite likely that inherent in the very difficulties that brought many clients to counseling in the first place is an inability to make effective interpersonal discriminations." If substantiated, this conclusion vitiates some of the other research in this area. It suggests that some clients may perceive the characteristics they desire from their therapists, even when these therapists do not appear to others to evidence them.

A number of worthwhile characteristics have been mentioned by therapists as attributes of the good therapist. He is not too anxious (Yulis and Kiesler, 1968); his emotional warmth is controlled (Frank, 1961, p. 130); so long as he is being himself (genuine), he can make jokes, be impudent, and act inconsistently in order to give his client a jolt (Fisher, 1965); he is well adjusted and has experience (Bergin, 1966); and he has a sense of humor, a zestful and energetic response to life, self-confidence, and optimism (Morgan, 1961; Frank, 1961, p. 141; Rosenthal, 1966). Moreover, he is viewed by his clients as influential or powerful so that what he has to say is regarded as persuasive (Truax, Fine, Moravec, and Millis, 1968). In short, the good therapist seems to be what most therapists believe he should be.

Yet in reality is the good therapist, even to other therapists, so clearly and so easily defined? Hardly. Although it is possible to agree that a good therapist is understanding and that this attribute is the *sine qua non* of the professional, a given response may seem understanding within one theoretical framework, and superficial or incorrect within another. These differences in understanding are not confined solely to interpretations and comments. They pervade the entire appraisal of a case. Thus therapists differ in their attitudes, their handling of specific symptoms, and their evaluation of the results of treatment. A psychoanalyst might very well consider clients whose behavior has been modified by a therapist who used desensitization as unimproved. Or one analyst may find the work of another analyst hasty and lacking in thoroughness. The same client may be thought of as improved and with no further need for therapy by the proponents of one system, while some of their colleagues may be convinced that the treatment process has not even begun. *Therefore what unites the various approaches is not any common understanding of particular behaviors, but the insistence that the therapists have an understanding that can be communicated to their clients.* This conclusion is supported by the studies of Strupp and Sundland and Barker.

Strupp (1958) found sizable differences between the attitudes and practices of psychoanalytic and Rogerian therapists. The Rogerians were reluctant to set a prescribed plan for treatment and to think of themselves as guided by fixed and definite goals. When compared with the analysts, they viewed their clients more favorably and tended to be more optimistic about the outcome of their cases. Their major concern was to promote the person's acceptance of himself, and by so doing to develop his potentialities more fully. In contrast, the psychoanalytic therapists placed more importance on the formulation of a treatment plan and on making decisions about the goals that were to be pursued. Their prognoses were more guarded than those of the Rogerians, as one would expect from the emphasis of psychoanalytic theory on the past, the repetition compulsion, and resistances. Further, the analytic therapists saw as one of their major tasks that of imparting insight, of helping the individual integrate what had happened to him before with his present personality functioning.

Sundland and Barker (1962) obtained similar results. They mailed Therapist Orientation Questionnaires to 400 psychologists who listed psychotherapy as a first or second interest in their biographical entries in the *APA 1959 Directory*. Returns were received from 139 therapists. An analysis of the responses disclosed two major orientations among the respondents. One, the "analytic," emphasized an understanding of unconscious processes, the planning of treatment, and the placing of restrictions on the therapist's spontaneity. The other, the "experiential," stressed the importance of the therapist's being spontaneous, of his having personality characteristics deemed appropriate for his role, of his attention to conscious processes, and of his willingness to take a relatively unplanned approach to treatment. Predictably, therapists who identified themselves as Freudian tended to have an "analytic" orientation, Rogerians tended to be "experiential," while those who claimed to be Sullivanians occupied an intermediate position between those two poles. Moreover, experienced therapists gave responses to these questions that were more similar to those of inexperienced therapists of their own orientation than they were to those of other experienced therapists; this indicated that in these particular matters the disagreements among therapists are pronounced and lasting.

These findings and those of Fiedler's are not as incompatible as they might at first seem. In point of fact, there are similarities and there are differences among therapists, and the kinship, for example, in terms of liberal values and political beliefs, is probably more pronounced than it is among people in general. Therapists agree to a large extent on matters of principle, though they disagree, again to a large extent, on practices and particulars.

The question of training illustrates the latter generalization. All therapists would agree that some training is important in the development of professionals who are to engage in the practice of psychotherapy. However, the content and the duration of that training are apt to elicit a considerable diversity of opinion. It is possible to argue that very little formal training is necessary, a position that does not enjoy too much favor among therapists who are mindful of the responsibilities that psychotherapy can impose. It could also be argued, with perhaps equal conviction and eloquence, that many years of study and supervision are needed.

When the assumptions underlying the different points of view are examined, they can be traced to the differences between various disciplines in beliefs about human nature and pathology. These beliefs have profound consequences, as will be discussed further in the next chapter, not only for clients, but also for members and prospective members of the profession. The complexities of a theory, which can be derived from its concept of man, its anthropomeliorism, determine the ease (its obviousness) with which it can be assimilated and accepted, both by the public and the profession.

Furthermore, professional organizations set standards to be met for their recognition, with demands that are different and by no means negligible. The majority of psychiatric social workers are required to have two years of graduate work and masters' degrees; clinical psychologists must take at least four years of graduate school before receiving their doctorates; and psychiatrists must have a medical education, then an internship, and then a residency, or about eight years of graduate work until they can practice with any independence. While these different investments of time are reflected in different salaries, it has yet to be demonstrated that they are reflected in psychotherapists of different levels of effectiveness. Nevertheless, although it is acknowledged that the length of preparation can detour prospective therapists from one field to another, and although the relevance of much of the medical training in psychiatry is not apparent to its practitioners (Mariner, 1967), and despite the clamor of the public for service, the arduous process of training therapists is little changed from what it was since such training began.

This lengthy and demanding process is made even more stringent in some systems by stipulations that those who would learn a particular method of psychotherapy must themselves experience its benefits. Outstanding in this regard, both in its insistence that this condition be met and in the number of years it takes to meet it, is psychoanalysis, a tradition that owes its origin to the dramatic departure from Freud's teachings of some of his most trusted pupils.

The ostensible advantages of psychotherapy for psychotherapists are many: (a) greater understanding of others follows from greater understanding of oneself; (b) the appreciation of the theory and its techniques is enhanced when one can experience its personal relevance; (c) the method and its impact are vividly demonstrated; (d) presumably, the therapist can be more empathic about the feelings of the client if he has lived through a similar situation; (e) although not undertaken because of any dire need, the candidate should find his own psychological functioning improved; and finally (f) the treatment should eliminate, or bring into awareness where they can be dealt with sensibly, derivatives of conflicts that might interfere with one's functioning as a therapist. These are advantages not to be lightly dismissed. Yet there is no study to show that therapists who have had psychotherapy are more effective than therapists who have not. In addition, there is little interest these days in demonstrating how fine a therapist one can become by long and conscientious preparation and study. Very much the opposite. At present, the question that is asked is how little training and information can one have and still get by as a psychotherapist.

There have been a number of studies and demonstration projects that have addressed themselves, at least in part, to that question. The effect that this array of evidence has on the members of the profession, whether they regard it as ridiculous and in the long run wasteful or sobering and a sign of great potential usefulness, depends on the understanding that they have of human behavior, and hence psychotherapy. Those who have a firm belief in the flexibility, strength, and capacity for growth of the individual can be expected to see less of a need for lengthy training. Carl Rogers, who is well known for espousing just such a belief, has argued, in a stand that is consistent with his convictions, that therapists can be trained to a satisfactory degree of competence in as little as two days: "If the therapeutic orientation is permissive and nonprobing, if the instructional approach is nonauthoritative and encourages the student to go at his own pace, then we do not need to fear that 'a little learning is a dangerous thing.' There are various degrees of therapeutic training which can be effectively used" (Rogers, 1951).

The point is that these studies arouse consternation in some therapists and enthusiasm in others, depending on their anthropomeliorism. In one of the first of these demonstrations, a training program conducted under the auspices of the National Institute of Mental Health tried to prepare housewives to serve as therapists (Pines, 1962). Two factors involved in this program merit emphasis. The housewives were a select group, composed mainly of college graduates, and even some women who had gone on to earn advanced degrees. They were not the run-of-the-mill housewife, complete with feather duster, apron, and mixing bowl. Second, the training program in psychotherapy that they received was as fine as most, undoubtedly better than some, programs provided for the training of professionals. Accordingly, it is not too discomfitting to learn that after several months of intensive training and supervision in the practice of psychotherapy, these women were able to function quite satisfactorily as therapists, at least in the limited sense of being able to communicate with clients so as to be of help to them.

The research that has followed has been similar, the variations being in how little training was received by what surprising group of people. Klein and Zax (1965) thrust college students taking a course in abnormal psychology, without too much ado, into a mental hospital where they were supposed to interact with chronic patients. Armed with good intentions and a wish to do well for their fellow man, these students floundered and fussed, but everyone seemed to benefit from the experience. The patients seemed to the hospital staff to have been "brought out of their shells" somewhat, while the students gained in sensitivity to their own feelings and those of the persons with whom they interacted.

Cowen and his colleagues (1966) took warm, friendly mothers, gave them some training in being helpful to teachers and pupils, and introduced them into the classroom or school to aid in the care of the children. Here the special interest of the investigators was to determine if the mothers would improve the mental health climate of the school, and thus prevent the appearance, or reduce the expected incidence, of emotional disturbances among the youngsters (primary prevention). The results were most encouraging. The teacher-moms or teacher-aides apparently had a salubrious effect since the children who had contacts with them were, on a number of measures, better adjusted than a comparable group that did not.

Hobbs (1966) reported that teachers can aid emotionally disturbed children in their overall adjustment when the effort is made to meet their psycho-educational needs; the innovative aspects of this study were that the children were not seen in "psychotherapy" and that the teachers carried the major responsibility for improving their condition. Tolor (1968) found that subprofessional "social counselors" who worked with 25 disturbed children in short-term treatment could have significant favorable effects on their emotional control and feelings of confidence about school. As a final example, and one that is perhaps a trifle more in keeping with these results than is necessary, is the study by Poser (1966). He analyzed the outcomes of the group therapy of 295 chronic schizophrenics (all male patients) and discovered that there had been somewhat better improvement, as measured on certain tests, for those who were treated by untrained therapists (all female) than for those treated by trained therapists (psychiatrists and psychiatric social workers of both sexes). This much may prudently be concluded about training:

1. There is no particular theoretical program that has to be taught in order to produce therapists who are effective because there is no particular understanding about human behavior, which alone comprehends and guides all psychotherapists in producing constructive changes. This does *not* mean that training is unimportant. It means that training can be flexible, that it can be narrowed or broadened, depending on the limits of the purposes we wish it to serve and the understanding of human behavior we deem it advisable to impart.

2. Persons can be trained to function specifically as "psychotherapists" in less time than it takes to train clinical psychologists, psychiatric social workers, and psychiatrists. This is so simply because the training of professionals equips them to perform a variety of skilled tasks including those of psychotherapy, and it provides them with a body of knowledge that extends beyond that field of interest.

3. To the extent that we desire to produce persons trained only to provide psychotherapy and to the extent that our concept of what constitutes help for the client is broad, we can cut into the length of training and comfortably reduce it.

4. Improvements in the person's psychological adjustment can be brought about by contacts with friendly, eager-to-be-helpful individuals. Such contacts have just been described as therapeutic, although they are not necessarily psychotherapy. However, putting that point aside for the moment, the concern that is often expressed within this context is how assistance can be given to those who seem to be inaccessible to professionals. The key to this problem seems to be whether the person offering the help can be accepted by the person who is supposed to receive it. There are times when professionals cannot be accepted, even by middle- and upper-class clients, when their presence is threatening and offensive, rather than reassuring. This means not only that nonprofessionals can be therapeutic, but also that so long as attempts are made to extend assistance to all whom it is felt are in need of it, nonprofessionals may be the only way for providing some form of this aid. Again, the aid provided may not be psychotherapy, even though it may be therapeutic.

Thus far in describing the "good therapist" it has been noted that his qualities of being understanding and trained are not delineated in such a way as to be definitive for the profession as a whole. Unfortunately, this holds true for many of his other attributes as well.

What may appear to be an instance of genuineness to Carl Rogers may appear to be an example of countertransference to psychoanalytic therapists. For example, in the film used by Shostram and Riley (1966), the young, attractive female client comments to Rogers that she would have liked to have had a father like him. To this Rogers responds that he would have been pleased to have her as a daughter. This remark, which Rogers explained in an epilogue as being a genuine expression of his feelings, draws expressions of dismay from audiences of professionals who do not share his orientation. They consider it a serious breach of psychotherapeutic practice.

Therapists agree that their expression of personal feelings in the hour can be appropriate, but only under these conditions: (a) their emotions are modulated and under control; (b) their emotional response is in reaction to what the client is saying and doing; and (c) the primary purpose of disclosing their feelings is that this is in the service of the client. They also agree that the therapist's self-expression would be inappropriate when it is extreme and uncontrolled, unrelated to what the client has said or done, and intended mainly to serve the needs of the therapist. But they do not agree on when these conditions exist.

How is one to reconcile the importance that therapists like Rogers ascribe to the personal nature of the therapeutic relationship with the attitude expressed by therapists like Sullivan (1954): "From beginning to end, to the best of his ability, the psychiatrist tries to avoid being involved as a person—even as a dear and wonderful person—and keeps to the business of being an *expert*"?

How can one make sense of the fact that some therapists believe their success is because of their acceptance of the client and their creation of a situation in which he can feel free, while other therapists think they are helpful when they are directive and authoritarian (Moss, 1967)?

What do therapists who strive to enable their clients to view the world without distortions have in common with therapists who see themselves fostering delusions (Masserman, 1953)?

In a general way, all of these therapists believe they are good therapists. They seek to be understanding, though they differ on what it actually means when one is understanding. They wish to be helpful; surely they do not aim to be harmful. They believe that they respect their clients; it is doubtful that they ever set out to be maliciously rude. Yet they are also different, and it would be an error to ignore their differences (Kiesler, 1966).

When these differences are examined, it is found that therapists are not equally interested in helping everyone, nor are they equally effective with the same clients, even under circumstances where they believe they are making use of the same form of psychotherapy. We shall now consider this line of research, studies that ask: "*What* treatment, by *whom,* is most effective for *this* individual with *that* specific problem, and under *which* set of circumstances?" (Paul, 1967).

THE GOOD THERAPIST OR THE APPROPRIATE THERAPIST

The most obvious basis for matching a particular therapist to a particular client is similarity. However, similarity is possible along a long line of variables. To quote from a conclusion drawn from research in the field of marriage: "Mates are selected from a field of eligibles. This field is determined by homogamy as to race, ethnic origin, social class, age, religion, and by residential propinquity" (Thorp, 1963). It seems safe for us to discount the significance of residential propinquity in this area, but the other variables could be of importance.

One suggestion is that the helping person be someone who has recovered from the disorder he is trying to treat, for example, former schizophrenics working with schizophrenic patients (Rosen, 1953). Further, it is well known that clients with some disturbances respond favorably only to those who have had similar problems. Alcoholics Anonymous comes readily to mind as a group that has experienced much success in helping alcoholics help alcoholics, and organizations based on the same principles exist that aid persons suffering from narcotics addiction and obesity. Many professionals candidly admit that they cannot invest the same time and effort that seems to be so willingly given by nonprofessionals.

Moreover, there are indications that even given a willingness of professionals to invest heavily of their energies, some clients respond better to those who know from first-hand experience a little of how they feel. *Time* (1967) described a situation in which reformed alcoholics, working for the Philadelphia Diagnostic and Relocation Service, were far more successful relocating derelicts in Philadelphia's Skid Row than were graduate students. And acting on the basis of the same impression, Pfeiffer (1967) has suggested that the spontaneous relationships that develop among patients in a mental hospital might well be guided by the staff so that the patients could function as intermediate therapists.

The wisdom of recruiting professionals from the legions of recovered clients is debatable, and it can be said without being thought excessively conservative that they are unlikely to be a major source of manpower.

Nevertheless, the dedication of these nonprofessionals, who recognize that they themselves gain by serving as an example to others, cannot be disputed. Fortunately, they exist. Accordingly, matching on the basis of shared suffering is more likely to be with a nonprofessional "therapist" than with one who is a professional, and it is very doubtful that trainees would be encouraged to enrich their backgrounds by undergoing emotional disturbances, despite the fact that many are convinced that such is an incidental purpose of advanced study.

An unsuspected, or at least not openly discussed, variable for matching used to be socioeconomic status. Middle-class therapists would pair themselves off in individual therapy with middle- or upper-class clients, and find themselves accused of being discriminatory against the poor. Without doubt they still pair themselves off in this way, although it is not clear to what extent this may be a rational decision.

What is fairly well established is that the good client has not been completely eradicated from the minds of psychotherapists. Although they intend to deal with people impartially on the basis of race and social position, they discriminate among their clients according to criteria that they believe are relevant for making decisions about the best form of psychotherapy.

The good client, the one who is considered most suitable for long-term individual psychotherapy, is, again, the intelligent person who seeks assistance in growing to understand his feelings and problems, the fellow who is dissatisfied with himself and his current life-situation, or the individual who experiences some anxiety about the adequacy of his adjustment. But these characteristics are not randomly distributed throughout the social classes. Quite the contrary. They tend to be associated with middle- and upper-class clients.

In striking contrast to the attributes of the good client are those found to predominate among members of the lower class: authoritarian, not democratic, orientation; anti-introspective character, that is, an aversion to examining their feelings and giving thought to the origins of their behavior in their life history; not being particularly receptive to the values of intensive psychotherapy, for example, self-actualization; for some not-so-strange reason feeling abused, mistreated, and at the mercy of forces that arbitrarily control their destiny; and, perhaps, most distressing, not having favorable attitudes toward psychiatrists (Jones and Kahn, 1964). How much of this is genuine, and how much of it is superficial or a hostile reaction to the investigators is difficult to say.

Aside from the disenchanting attitudes he may encounter when the therapist sees a lower-class client, he also finds a greater incidence of severe pathology. Here too the argument goes round and round. Do lower-class clients fall victim to the most serious disturbances, or do middle-class therapists unwittingly make diagnoses that are too harsh because they fail to understand and be sympathetic to persons of low socio-economic status? Whatever the reason may be, schizophrenia and personality disorders are diagnosed at a higher rate in the lower class (Dohrenwend and Dohrenwend, 1967). And these diagnoses are not without their consequences for treatment.

As might be expected, there is a relationship between the diagnosis and the type of treatment prescribed. In general, the more severe the disturbance is though to be, the more likely it is for the primary goal of treatment to be the relief of symptoms (Michaux and Lorr, 1961). Therefore, the lower-class client, who tends to be judged more seriously disturbed, tends to receive what is referred to as "directive treatment" (Frank, 1961, p. 7), an authoritarian approach in which the therapist tries to alleviate symptoms by drugs, advice, environmental manipulations, or making use of any other possibly effective measure that will not take up too much of his time.

But that is not all. Intelligence and education are also related to social class, with those in the lower being less educated and scoring lower on intelligence tests than those in the higher classes. Once again, these are characteristics that do not make the lower-class client particularly appealing to therapists who are making selections for individual psychotherapy.

Further, there are suggestions that there are other qualities associated with the good client that are more closely related to middle and upper classes than to the lower. The good client is probably dependent, not in the sense in which that term is applied to the lower class, but in the way in which it is used by Sears et al. (1953, 1957), a learned motivational system that is evidenced by help-seeking, attention-seeking, and approval-seeking behaviors. In other words, it is an active form of dependency in which the person tries to act and to express beliefs that will be pleasing to authority and give credence to his good intentions and cooperation; while the dependency ascribed to the lower class is passive, a hopeless resignation that complains about what is being done or just accepts it.

Connections can also be seen between Sears' concept of dependency and Crowne and Marlowe's (1960) concept of social desirability, a need to obtain approval by giving responses that are culturally appropriate and acceptable. Both probably are associated with middle, not low, socioeconomic status, and both seem to be characteristics associated with successful psychotherapy. Dependency has been found to be positively related to continuation in psychotherapy (Winder et al., 1962); and it seems likely to be tied in with the qualities of the good client as being a person who regards the therapist as an esteemed expert, a respected authority figure whose comments and understanding are to be highly valued (Rogers,

1942). Social desirability, in addition to its obvious implications for expressing what will be pleasing to the therapist, was discovered to have a bearing on responsiveness to verbal conditioning; persons who had a strong need for social approval produced significantly more statements favorable to themselves when they were verbally rewarded for doing so than did persons whose need for social approval was low (Marlowe, 1962).

Since professional therapists are members of the middle and upper classes, it does not seem too daring to suppose that their needs are similar to those of their middle- and upper-class clients. Thus middle-class client and therapist can be mutually rewarding, both can function in ways that satisfy their needs to be pleasing in a kind of compatible or symbiotic relationship. The therapist rewards the client, and the client rewards the therapist by showing appreciation for his skill and dedicated efforts, by paying his bills, and by being interested in what interests the therapist. Meanwhile, the typical lower-class client sits passively or complains about physical problems or environmental conditions, which makes the therapist feel unhappy because there is not much that he believes he can do about them. Small wonder that the therapist opts for the middle- and upper-class client for long-term individual psychotherapy, where the aim is to elicit feelings and memories in order to bring about a general improvement in self-understanding and functioning.

For some time it has been fruitlessly debated whether middle-class therapists (teachers, authorities, power structure, etc.) have a biased and stereotypic view of their lower-class clients (a good many of them do, and a good many of them also have a biased and stereotypic view of their middle- and upper-class clients) or whether lower-class clients have values and attitudes and disturbances that contraindicate long-term psychotherapy. Moreover, it has been argued that the poor, in addition to their other deprivations, are being deprived of the best therapy available and the benefits of actualizing themselves; instead, they are being offered a palliative therapy, a way of "cooling it" without really doing too much about their emotional disturbances. In defense of the therapists, it is contended that the poor are so mired in reality problems that self-actualization is about the least of their needs, worries, or concerns; that the treatment offered *is* the best therapy under the circumstances; and that members of the lower class are not blameless, that is, by their suspiciousness and defensiveness when being evaluated for treatment they have made some contribution to any misunderstandings that have arisen.

It is pointless to continue these arguments. That the poor are capable of responding to and deriving benefit from a psychotherapeutic relationship has been demonstrated by the work of Hertha Riese (1962) and James McMahon (1964). However, it would be absurd to regard the published reports, as represented by these two, as the sum total of the evidence in support of individual psychotherapy for members of the lower class. For years clinics have been in operation providing psychotherapy to the poor. The breathless discoveries of impoverished children and laborers responding to therapy are thus somewhat disheartening to professionals who have labored long in this area, and who gave little thought to the possibility that their colleagues harbored unfavorable stereotypes and misconceptions. Ironically, much of the heated dialogue for liberal attitudes promotes yet another group of stereotypes. Certainly therapists are best advised to meet each of their clients, regardless of socioeconomic status, with patience, flexibility, respect, and the knowledge that this person is an individual who may depart from the norms.

The situation as it exists today is not especially promising for therapists who seek to work with the poor and who are sensitive to rebuffs. If nothing else, the Black Power movement has made whites and blacks fully conscious of racial differences between them; and it has made hate so fashionable that even Negroes who do not feel hostility, feel an obligation to be vituperative.

Thus, at present, there is a polarization of racial attitudes, which makes it difficult not only for whites to deal with blacks, but also for blacks to deal with whites. This is something that shall pass, and certainly it is something that can be handled in psychotherapy so long as the therapist is not awed by it and regards it for what it is, an attitude or feeling of the client that should not be allowed to obstruct their aims for treatment.

Nevertheless, the current interest is not so much in seeing whether lower-class clients are really amenable to individual psychotherapy if therapists would redouble their efforts to be of help to them. The shortage of professionals is so severe that there is little pressure in that direction. Nor is it feasible to match clients with professionals on the basis of race, or for that matter sex. Less than 1% of the psychologists and psychiatrists in the United States are Negroes; over 75% of the 11,560 psychologists working in the field of mental health are men (NIMH, 1966). What is of interest is developing the use of nonprofessionals to be of assistance.

These nonprofessionals have, for the most part, been recruited from the ranks of the poor. They have not functioned, at least to their way of thinking, as therapists. Instead, they have been employed most often as helpful neighbors, acquainting people with community resources, aiding them to meet emergencies, and listening to their troubles. The reports about their usefulness have tended to be favorable and, as is true of innovations, enthusiastic.

If nonprofessionals were to perform therapeutic roles more frequently, there is a suggestion from a study by Carkhuff and Pierce (1967) that they should be matched with clients of their own race. The investigators had four lay therapists conduct an initial interview with four schizophrenic patients. Both therapists and patients were composed of one Negro upper class, one white upper-class, one Negro lower-class, and one white lower-class member. The results were that there were significant differences in depth of self-exploration depending on whether the race of client and therapist was the same. Considering that the study took place in the South, the times in which we live, and the clients being schizophrenic, the findings should be taken with caution.

It would seem that, given a competent therapist who would be in contact with a client over an extended period of time, the similarities between the two participants in race and socioeconomic status would be irrelevant. However, it must be recognized that therapists do not always measure up to their ideals, that clients walk out after one or two interviews never to return, that things occasionally fall apart, and that the world is less than perfect. Therefore, if it is desired to increase the probability of success, it would be sensible to match, insofar as possible, therapist and client on the basis of race and social class, with one stipulation: it should be kept in mind that lower-class clients who wish psychotherapy may prefer to be seen by professionals, even middle- and upper-class ones.

Religion is not often mentioned as a matching variable, but there are times when it would be appropriate to pair a therapist and client of the same religion. The person may have conflicts about his faith that are discussed best with someone who has some knowledge of the issues involved, or the person may be prejudiced against certain religions and immediately dislike therapists who belong to them. It also happens that the client may prefer to have a therapist who does not share his religion so that he can express his doubts about his faith frankly. Ordinarily the matter is not discussed, and it is assumed that the client is not biased, or that if he is, the therapist can deal with it so that it does not disrupt the treatment. This presumption has about as much validity as any other.

The sex of the therapist can be an important matching variable. As was mentioned earlier, there are not too many female psychologists and psychiatrists, although women outnumber men in the field of psychiatric social work. Clinical impressions suggest that a female therapist may be indicated when the client is an adolescent girl or when the client has intense feelings of hostility toward men. The need for a male therapist seems to exist with adolescent males and clients who have animosities toward mother figures. Certain forms of disturbance, those in which the gratification of dependency needs play a significant role, for example, alcoholism and schizophrenia, appear to be handled more successfully by female therapists (Wolberg, 1967, p. 502). One would also suppose that the discussion of some problems, especially sexual difficulties, would be easier if the therapist and client were of the same sex. Yet there does not seem to be any research evidence to shed light on these matters; thus decisions are made on the basis of the above clinical impressions and the hope that the therapist's skill will enable him to overcome any obstacles.

Despite all the talk about generation gaps, age is in about the same category as sex, insofar as its relevance has been studied. It seems reasonable to expect that some clients would respond better to older or younger therapists. Particularly now, when adolescents are told so frequently by the mass media that they are possessed of values and beliefs quite different from their elders, they might be better "turned on" by a therapist who is young. On the other hand, a client struggling with concerns about middle age or approaching senility may feel more comfortable with a therapist who is old. The last statement of the preceding paragraph may now also be read here.

Similarity of personality characteristics between therapist and client has been investigated. A study by Carson and Heine (1962) demonstrated that success in psychotherapy, as measured by the ratings of supervising psychiatrists of the treatment outcomes, varied significantly with similarity in the shape of MMPI profiles of client and therapist. Interestingly, the relationship was curvilinear. Extreme similarity and extreme dissimilarity both appeared to affect the treatment process adversely. In explaining their findings, Carson and Heine speculated that perhaps too close a correspondence in personality functioning between therapist and client made it difficult for the two participants to maintain the proper psychological distance. However, differences in personality between them that were too great led to problems for the therapist in being sufficiently understanding and sensitive to his client.

Another study, by Mendelsohn and Rankin (1969), lends some support to the notion that matching of therapist and client can be a significant means to facilitate therapeutic success. This was an elaborate piece of research in which counseling was restricted to no more than eight interviews, and in which differences were found only for female clients. Nevertheless, the results indicated, somewhat as in the Carson and Heine study, that when therapist and client had compatible systems of needs that promoted closeness, the therapeutic process was hampered. But when female clients and their therapists had compatible needs about control, for example, a female client who wanted to be controlled and a therapist who wished to be controlling, a positive relationship was found to treatment outcome. It would be hazardous to generalize too much from this study, though it does seem safe to say that it argues against a willy-nilly assignment of therapist to client.

Control was measured by Mendelsohn and Rankin by means of the Fundamental Interpersonal Relations Orientation Behavior scale. Another measure of control, the Internal-External (I-E) scale (Rotter, Liverant, and Crowne, 1961), concerns itself with a different aspect of this dimension. The scale consists of 29 statements to which the person responds by indicating whether he agrees with the sentiment expressed. The statements attempt to assess the individual's beliefs about the determination of his behavior. Does he believe that what happens to him comes about because of his own actions and decisions (Internal control)? Or does he believe that his behavior is governed by outside forces, environmental pressures and events, fate, chance, and significant others (External control)? His convictions about the matter of control appear to be an important characteristic of his personality, one that has a bearing on significant other beliefs and behaviors (Lefcourt, 1966).

Males who score high on Internal control, but not females, seem to do better on intelligence test scores and achievement in school. For both sexes, Internal control seems to be positively related to hopefulness, and we have already noted the importance ascribed to that dimension in psychotherapy. External control has been found to be associated with scores on the California F Scale (a measure of authoritarianism), with feelings of hopelessness and resignation, and with Negroes rather than whites (Lefcourt, 1966; Rotter, 1966). In short, it would appear that I-E scores are very much related to socioeconomic status or class, with poor people feeling as they do that they have little to say about what happens to them. Nevertheless, given clients of a particular social class, the prediction would be that I-score clients would respond better to therapy than E-score clients. Although this hypothesis has not been tested as yet, there are indications that it would be supported.

Hersch and Scheibe (1967) did a study of college students who were either attending summer school or who were working on the chronic wards of a mental hospital. The students who were I scorers seemed to be less maladjusted than the E, and they described themselves in more positive terms, for example, as being active, independent, effective, achieving, powerful, and striving.

Tiffany (1967) studied 24 patients in a mental hospital. He found that those who were ready for discharge scored higher on I control than did the patients who had just been admitted. His findings further commend the I-E scale as a valid instrument, and they suggest that I scores would be related to positive self-concepts, adequate social adjustments, and success in treatment. It would be worthwhile to investigate the distribution of I-E scores among psychotherapists, to determine if I-control therapists are more effective than E, and to see what effects there might be in therapy when clients and therapists are matched on the I-E dimension.

The I-E scale is a promising device for selecting the appropriate therapist for a specific client. The theory of behavior behind it has not been discussed here, but there is a theory. However, there is no theoretical basis for the Whitehorn-Betz A-B scale. This scale came about empirically. It emerged from the authors' needs to develop some objective index for their conviction that: *"the doctor is the important, even crucial, factor in determining the outcome of treatment with schizophrenic patients"* (Betz, 1962).

Fourteen physicians who had approximately the same amount of experience in treating schizophrenics were divided into two groups on the basis of whether the rate of improvement for the patients they treated was more or less than 68%. The more successful group simply was labeled "A"; its physicians had treated 48 schizophrenics, of whom 36 or 75% had improved. The group composed of the less successful physicians was called "B"; its members had treated 52 schizophrenics, with improvement in only 14, or 27%. Now the problem was to see if the groups could be distinguished on the basis of criteria that were not specifically related to treatment outcomes.

In general, the typical A physician appeared to be more sensitive to the feelings of his patients than the B. He related to them as persons rather than as cases of pathology. Although he set limits on obnoxious behavior, he respected the spontaneous actions and remarks of his schizophrenic patients, and he himself tended to be spontaneous in the therapy hour. His role was an active one, in which by his attitude of friendly concern and interest a warm human relationship of trust was promoted.

The typical B physician was almost the opposite of the A. He tended to remain at a distance from his patients, and he viewed them with a clinical detachment. His role tended to be a passive one, and, as if he were absorbed in his study of pathology, he allowed obnoxious behavior to occur without making any effort to interfere with it. Yet his own aloof manner curtailed not only his own spontaneity, but that of his patients as well. The relationship that developed was that of lecturer or naturalist and object of study or instruction (Betz, 1967).

Despite these differences in personality characteristics, it was hoped that there might be some simple objective screening device that could reliably separate physicians into these two groups. The Strong Vocational Interest Inventory had been taken by a number of physicians, and there were test results for 15 A's and 11 B's. Perhaps there were significant differences in interests between them, even though all were members of the medical profession.

Happily, there turned out to be significant differences between A's and B's on the Strong. The A's scored higher than the B's for Lawyer and Certified Public Accountant, but they scored lower than the B's for Printer and Math Teacher. Further, an item analysis of the Strong indicated that just 23 of the 400 questions discriminated between the two groups. Not too much rhyme or reason could be made out of these differences. For example, the A's responded that they liked "Many women friends" and disliked "Mechanical Engineer"; while the B's liked "Carpenter" and disliked "Follow up subordinates effectively." Nevertheless, these 23 items were assembled, and together they comprised the Whitehorn-Betz A-B Scale; although at times Whitehorn and Betz made use of only ten items when an abbreviated version was desired for screening purposes.

The A-B Scale has found its way into a considerable body of research (Dublin, Elton, and Berzins, 1969) with results that become "curiouser and curiouser." McNair et al. (1962) used it to evaluate the effectiveness of therapist "types," but this time with a neurotic instead of a schizophrenic outpatient population. With neurotic clients, B therapists apparently were more effective than A. The investigators exhibited admirable restraint and resisted the temptation to make the obvious conclusion that A therapists do better with schizophrenics and B therapists do better with neurotics. What they did do was analyze their data further and direct their attention to the socioeconomic status of the neurotic and schizophrenic samples and the interests of the therapists.

The neurotic sample was made up largely of lower- or lower-middle-class clients; some 70% of the sample was of this social grouping. In contrast the schizophrenic sample was predominantly of a higher socioeconomic grouping, and only 30% of these clients were lower or lower-middle class. Since the B therapists evidenced an interest in skilled labor and technical activities (lower- and lower-middle-class occupations), McNair and his colleagues suggested that they, "had interests more in common with their patients, more similar life backgrounds, or were more familiar with the daily living problems encountered by their patients."

McNair, Callahan, and Lorr's interpretation of their data plumps for similarity between client and therapist. Moreover, it implies that the warm and distant relationships observed by Whitehorn and Betz were the artifacts of incompatible therapist-client matchings, and not direct functions of the therapists' personalities. Presumably, if their schizophrenic sample had been of lower-class background, the B therapists would have been more effective there too; or, considering how the groups came about in the first place, there would have been a shift between the memberships of the A and B therapists, the personality descriptions of the A's and B's would remain the same, but now the A's would score high for printer and math teacher and low for lawyer and certified public accountant. Note that being of the same socioeconomic status is not the relevant variable, since this was the case for the majority of patients and therapists in the Whitehorn-Betz studies; yet differences in outcome among therapists were found. The conclusion that emerges is that the chances for favorable treatment outcomes are enhanced when therapists are able to share their clients' values and interests, perhaps with some degree of enthusiasm. As Angyal put it: "I have often observed that when I am in a good resilient frame of mind my patients become more productive and in general work better in their sessions. This observation was confirmed in private conversations with other therapists" (Angyal, 1965).

But a study by Berzins, Friedman, and Seidman (1969) interprets what is relevant for the A-B variable quite differently. Their research tried to assess the relationship between the A-B scores of 60 male clients in a college clinic and their symptoms and expectations in the first therapy hour. The A clients tended to feel depressed, with the various symptoms associated with depression, for example, feelings of worthlessness, tearfulness, and inability to study. The B clients did not fall into any neat category of symptoms, but they appeared to express their anger more openly than the A's. As far as their role expectations in treatment were concerned, the A's wanted to do a good deal of the talking and to express their feelings, while the B's tended to expect the therapist to be directive, probing, and somewhat tutorial.

In discussing their data, Berzins, Friedman, and Seidman accept the personality descriptions of A and B therapists given by Betz as consistently true of all A and B therapists; and they accept McNair et al.'s finding that B therapists do better with neurotics, while implicitly rejecting the explanation that this was a function of similarity of interests between lower-class neurotics and B therapists. Instead, they put forth a hypothesis that complementarity on the A-B variable, not similarity, may mediate who is the effective therapist: ". . . the complementarity hypothesis leads to the prediction that A therapists would perform better with B patients, and B therapists—with A patients (than A's with A's and B's with B's)" (Berzins et al., 1969). The complementarity that they have in mind is in styles of interpersonal behaviors, for example, the rather passive B therapist with the active and eager-to-get-talking A client. What is brushed aside a bit is why the B client who wants to be told what to do should not do just fine with the B therapist who has a didactic style?

Another possible explanation for the results found to date is in the styles of the therapists' and the clients' expectations about what is the proper or desirable role for the therapist. Earlier research has indicated that lower-class clients favor a directive approach, and this might be true particularly when, as in the McNair study, treatment is limited to four months. Now the B therapists have been described as having two different clinical styles, instructional or passive (Betz, 1967); the former would seem to fit the needs of many lower-class clients, while the latter would correspond with what many informed people conceive to be the model functioning for psychoanalysts. It would be interesting to see if B therapists are effective with schizophrenic clients who wish a directive approach, and if A therapists are effective with neurotic clients who seek a warm, giving relationship.

Although there is still much to be done in the A-B area, this at least seems clear—the matching of therapist and client can be crucial in determining the success of psychotherapy. Certainly, these variables are ignored only at some cost, both to the client and to the person who with the best of intentions wishes to be of help to a fellow human being.

CONCLUSIONS

It has been suggested that psychotherapy be defined as the communication of person-related understanding, respect, and a wish to be of help. This examination of the therapist has yielded no evidence to compel that tentative definition to be modified. The therapist has been found to be a variable individual whose effectiveness depends less on the appraisals of his colleagues and more on the appraisals of his clients. What his clients want and expect have to be taken into account. Although broadly speaking therapists share in the importance they ascribe to certain characteristics, for example, being understanding, they disagree about the specifics of these characteristics and about their role in psychotherapy. Thus there are no qualities of the therapist that are definitive, and it is preferable to speak, not of a good therapist, but of an appropriate therapist for a particular client.

CHAPTER 5

An Examination of the Metasystems
of Psychotherapy

Everywhere the human soul stands between a hemisphere of light and another of
darkness; on the confines of the two everlasting hostile empires, necessity and free will.

Thomas Carlyle

The gift most precious to Creative Thought,
Most signal of God's bounties, and the one
After the pattern of His goodness wrought,
Was Freedom of the Will,—a benison
Wherewith all creatures of intelligence
Both were and are endowed, and they alone.

Dante Alighieri

There is no such thing as free will. The mind is induced to wish this or that by some
cause, and that cause is determined by another cause, and so on back to infinity.

Benedict Spinoza

Systems of psychotherapy have roots that draw deeply from their concept
of man. These beliefs subtly influence theories and decisions affecting individuals in treatment, and are explicitly stated as positions to challenge
the views of one or another group of professionals. For close to a century
the controversy about whether man has a free will has appeared in the
pages of psychology journals. For centuries before that, the question of
man's freedom had been a subject for lively and troubling discourse.

The Old Testament begins with man in the Garden of Eden, naked,
at one with nature, and free to do as he wishes, but with one restriction
—he must not eat the fruit of the tree of knowledge of good and evil.
As is well known, man yields to temptation, eats of the fruit, and is punished. One thing that this story makes clear is that people have long conceived of man as being free to choose whether to inhibit or to yield to his

impulses. When he elects to gratify himself without restraint or regard for the prohibitions that he knows exist, he must be prepared to suffer the consequences. And the consequences do come. Repeatedly throughout the Old Testament, man is punished for setting himself against what he knows he should do and for indulging himself in what he knows is wrong. With the exception of one family, Noah's, he is wiped out, man, woman, and child, in the flood. He is destroyed in Sodom and Gomorrah. He is swallowed up, slain, deprived of his fondest hope, humiliated, tortured, and driven from his homeland. He pays dearly for his knowledge of good and evil, and for his choice of the latter. But he also is rewarded, if not now, then perhaps in the future, when he chooses to do what is right. The choice, however, between immediate gratification and delayed rewards is his to make.

The ancient Greeks frequently depicted man as seeming to be free, but actually controlled by fate, by circumstances, by the whims and wishes of the gods. Oedipus thought he was free, but he did not choose to murder his father and marry his mother, nor did he do so knowingly. The full facts were hidden from him, as they often are from all of mankind. When Oedipus could see, he was blind to the incestuous relationship in which he was involved. When Oedipus was blind, he could see that no man can think of himself as fortunate until his death. The moral seemed plain to the Greeks. All men are unable to know what is right or wrong until they know all, and they never do know all. Therefore, man can only try his best to do what seems right to him at the time. His sense of being free is an illusion because his choices are based on incomplete knowledge, and the course of his life has been charted since long before his birth.

These two views of man have lived through the ages because they have made sense. One person walks with a God who is just, who punishes him when he decides to follow wickedness and who favors him when he elects to follow the path of righteousness. Another walks with a God who is omnipotent and omniscient, who has predestined all lives but who probably signals those he has selected for salvation by the goodness of their actions.

The theological concept of free will follows from a conviction about God's goodness and fair play. He would not inflict suffering capriciously, He could not cause pain wickedly and without provocation; therefore the punishments must be deserved. But in order for them to be deserved, in order for the person to be held accountable for his actions, he must have been free to choose between what was correct and what was not. If he were not free, then God would be punishing the person for something over which he had no control—which would not be fair—which would not be consistent with this concept of God.

But the Christian concept of God has also led some theologians to a belief in determinism. For God is all-powerful and all-knowing, and therefore not only does He know what each person will do, but He could alter their behaviors if He wished. What men do is thus God's will. It is part of a divine plan. From the narrow perspective of man's lifetime, what happens may seem incomprehensible and unjust. But from the perspective of eternity, things fall into their proper and correct places. However, the person may ask, why should he bother to be good since it has already been determined what he shall do and what rewards he shall receive? Only this. His being good is probably an indication of God's favor, while those who do evil appear to have been destined for the fires of hell.

From a secular point of view, the arguments for free will and determinism have been quite different from those of the theologians. The balance of this chapter will consist of a statement of representative secular positions, a consideration of the resolutions that have been proposed for this controversy, and a discussion of the issue's implications for psychotherapists and the definition of psychotherapy.

THE CASE FOR FREE WILL

It is sometimes argued that free will is a misnomer. What people are concerned with is not the freedom of an abstraction, the will, but the freedom of the individual or person. This distinction is usually understood by those who have devoted much thought to these matters, and they still use the term "free will." Accordingly, we shall use it too, although it should also be understood when we use it that we are referring to the individual, and not to a circumscribed aspect of his anatomy or functioning.

The most persuasive evidence for the belief in the existence of free will is phenomenological. Most people believe that they are free to make choices, and that freedom is a fact of their existence. After all, what could be more natural and obvious than for them to believe in their own freedom? Each day with its many opportunities for decisions and choice provides them with fresh evidence of their ability to judge each new situation on its own merits and then to decide alone on a course of action, upon giving rein to their preferences and to their tastes. There is little doubt that they seldom pause to give any thought to the notion that they are not free. Instead, they assume simply that they are free; that even under the most deplorable conditions of constraint, they preserve a certain degree of freedom that allows them to maintain some dignity, some sense of being a human, some ability to select among thoughts and actions.

When they do stop for a moment to reflect upon their own behavior, they obtain convincing proof of their freedom. They praise themselves and feel a sense of satisfaction for behavior that they believe has been correct and of fine quality. And conversely, they feel anger and unhappiness when they have made mistakes or failed to act in keeping with their own standards. In short, they feel responsible for their behavior, and not only do they reward and punish themselves for what they actually do, but also for what they feel and think.

Most people believe that virtually everything that they do is based, in the end, on their willingness to do that particular thing. This is not to imply that they do only what they find pleasurable, since for a variety of reasons they may select an alternative that is not immediately satisfying. However, it is to say that they feel they could have elected one plan over another for their own good reasons, and that they believe they could have made a very different choice if they had summoned up the courage or the wish. Inmates of concentration camps and prisoners of war still retain this sense of free will because they know that ultimately they could choose death rather than compliance. Thus virtually all individuals experience themselves as more or less carefully gathering information to help them to arrive at decisions, agonizing and taking pains during times when they weigh the merits of several alternatives; and often not knowing themselves which way they shall turn, until finally the suspense ends, and the moment comes when they arrive at a resolution of the problem.

The case for free will, for the belief that men are at liberty to decide what they want, rests on introspection, on the feeling that man controls his behavior. Given an individual who has this belief, it then is a fact of his existence. It is real, it exists for him. Of course, it may not actually be true, just as any other belief may have no foundation in reality. But if he is convinced of it, then it is true for him, and it is part of his reality. At the very least, it can be said that there is free will for each person who believes his will is free. "I am the master of my fate," wrote the poet W. E. Henley, "I am the captain of my soul." It is a belief that has existed down through the ages, and it is the cornerstone for man's belief in his uniqueness as a being in nature.

But the phenomenological reality of free will is not enough to satisfy everyone. To some moralists this is merely begging the issue. Free will must really exist or else people will not feel that they should be held responsible for their behavior. Essentially, what these moralists are saying is that if free will does not actually exist, then it is not fair to hold men accountable for their actions.

Similarly, some jurists will argue that free will must really exist, or else it would not be just to make men legally responsible for their actions. Both the moralist and the jurist are struggling with the problem that has bothered the theologian; but they have subsituted the goodness and wisdom of the state, society, and the law for the goodness and wisdom of God. It is not right to sanction or to punish someone for something over which he had no control. Therefore, since authorities do punish and criticize people, they must assume that the offenders did have control over their behavior, that they were free to act differently. Otherwise, the prisons and the penalties of the society would be a gross injustice. Otherwise they could not expect people to rise above their mean circumstances, they could not simply sit by and wonder why some individuals elect to live in poverty, they could not inflict suffering and death upon their fellow man without guilt or remorse.

Free will, it is argued, actually exists because so much of what is legally done is predicated on its actual existence and because it is needed for our existence. To do away with it would be to invite chaos, irresponsibility, and disorder. Those who would deny free will can be seen from this position as trying to deny their responsibility or their humanness. Their denial of free will is an escape, an excuse, a rationalization, probably done to avoid facing their own unwillingness to accept challenges and the burdens of their misdeeds. Free will is neither an illusion nor a bit of phenomenological reality. Free will does exist, as the essential attribute of man.

THE CASE FOR DETERMINISM

Even among those who argue strongly for free will, it is recognized that man is not always free. The question is to what extent he can be said to have some freedom. Everyone can readily acknowledge that there are restrictions on his freedom coming about through demands of his society or culture, through laws, and through obligations and attachments imposed by his possession of property. If we see a man driving a car toward a traffic signal that is red, we can be almost certain that he will bring his vehicle to a stop, regardless of his impatience and his contrary wishes.

However, these restrictions on man's behavior are seen as coming from without, as external to the individual. They are not thought to affect the person's ability to consider other choices and to wish to make them. Even though social demands may blot out the overt expression of alternatives to its prescribed patterns, they do not, to those who believe in free will, eliminate accountability, the responsibility of the person to act in accordance with what he knows to be true, reasonable, and right. The most totalitarian of regimes—and certainly Hitler's Germany fits that description—did not relieve individuals of their obligation to be human (as was demonstrated by the Nuremberg trials), which is to conceive of what is possible, to consider choices, and to try to do what personally seems to be correct.

Yet it is also readily acknowledged that there can be restraints on an individual's freedom that are subtle, and that are occasionally in conflict with the professed aims of the society. Within the culture of the United States, great value is placed on the development of uniqueness, self-expression, and creative thought. Further, this society is relatively free so that there appears to be little external justification for any failure to grow and to express one's individuality. Yet the demands for conformity in dress, manner, the arts, political opinions, and what have you are nevertheless great. And they are made even more poignant because here the freedom to proclaim one's difference ostensibly exists, while the fear of alienating one's fellow man by asserting how one differs from him seems to know no national boundaries. Granting, then, that these subtle pressures exist, that people may feel torn between an acute consciousness of both the rewards and the painfulness of conformity but that in the main they appear to have decided to go along with the styles and fashions of the crowd, still those who believe in free will insist that the person could choose to go his own original way.

To the determinists, free will is solely an illusion, though perhaps to some an interesting and important one. They believe that man is not at liberty to act independent of his antecedent conditions, any more than anything else in this universe is. Thus just as man's uniqueness in nature is closely associated with the concept of free will, so the determinists argue for man's continuity with other forms of life.

Although modern determinists assert that every event, including human behavior, could be understood and predicted if we were completely aware of all that is relevant that exists before it occurs, they do not usually go on to draw the same logical, but dazzling, implications of their predecessors. Many early determinists claimed that if all follows from what has happened, then the course of our lives and of all history has already been determined. The tempo of events is merely the falling of pieces that inevitably must fall; we might call this the Domino Corollary of determinism. And if we take seriously the notion that what takes place today and tomorrow was set into inexorable motion long, long ago, it follows that there is no real reason to feel responsible for our behavior. However, this last conclusion is most objectionable not only to those who believe in free will, but also to some determinists. The logical consequences of this conclusion appear to be so mischievous that Grünbaum, who allied himself with determinism, undermined his position in attempting to explain it away: ". . . neither the causes of our desires nor psychological laws, which state under what conditions our desires arise, compel us in any way to act in a manner contrary to our own will" (Grünbaum, 1953).

But even without the issue of people assuming a stance of irresponsibility if determinism were widespread, the very concept of predictability when applied to human behavior arouses indignation. That what a man will do should be known to someone else when he himself may still be undecided strikes many individuals as preposterous, if not somewhat frightening. Yet the determinists reply that despite the protests of individuality and uniqueness, creativity, and setting forth anew, man's actions follow orderly sequences. They point out that regularities to conduct do exist; that under specifiable conditions a person's actions are governed mainly by cultural demands, laws, conventions, etiquette, and so on. They note that it is no great feat to predict that the conversation and general behavior at a wedding party will be cheerful and superficial, but at a funeral it will be subdued and solemn. Obviously, given knowledge about a culture, it can be predicted how most people who subscribe to that culture will respond to certain sets of circumstances (for example, the Labor Day weekend) and to certain stimuli (the playing of The Star Spangled Banner).

In addition, the determinists might generalize a bit further by mentioning gently that there is merit in what Leo Tolstoy had to say about the matter of free will. Tolstoy argued that man's behavior is free only when he does not see it as of any consequence to others. Alone in a room he may scratch if and where he wishes, lift his hand if he chooses, and do what he would. But in company or when his actions have a bearing on others, his freedom is curtailed. He cannot scratch his body wherever it may itch, and he cannot lift his hands if in so doing they strike someone else. And if the company is mixed, his freedom is restricted even more. Men have duties, obligations, and impressions they wish to create and fulfill. Taken all in all, most people would find it hard to fault Tolstoy's (1938) conclusion: ". . . we cannot but see that the more abstract and therefore the less connected with the activities of others our activity is, the more free it is; and on the contrary, the more our activity is connected with other people the less free it is."

An implication of Tolstoy's argument is that the more knowledge people have of social conventions and expectations, the less freedom they would feel they have. Their awareness of what is expected of them narrows the range of behaviors that they would be comfortable in expressing to a slender band. Since ordinarily most persons try to do what is fitting and proper, it is not uncommon for them to feel that the customs and rules hamper them. This is conformity, in its suffocating sense.

However, it is also possible to argue that awareness of the culture increases the range of choices. Speaking generally, it has been asserted that knowledge frees, while ignorance binds. By being fully informed about what is involved in a state of affairs and of all the possible ways in which one might deal with it, people increase the number of options available to them, and thus their freedom to implement their choices. This was the point emphasized by Thomas Aquinas (Durant, 1950). If an individual does not perceive a situation correctly, if his perceptions of his judgments are distorted by prejudices and false beliefs and opinions, then to a certain extent he is impeded in arriving at a legitimate course of action. Moreover, it may be said that to the extent that people are ignorant of alternatives and the means or skills to perform them, then to that extent is their freedom curtailed. Man's freedom, according to Aquinas, is a direct function of his knowledge, not only when he is clearly aware of his limitations, but also when he might incorrectly believe that he has dealt with a situation competently.

That knowledge can be perceived as both liberating and binding is a paradox associated with freedom, which is intrinsic to it, and which leads to the conclusion that man's being free has no foundation in the real world, but is solely a matter of the individual's perception. Tolstoy, among others, sees man's awareness of the rules and conventions of society as hampering his freedom. He perceives man's natural inclinations and impulses being inhibited by his social interests and concerns. Yet Aquinas, also correctly, points out that the more alternatives man recognizes and the more he is aware of what he could do in a given situation, the greater is his freedom of action. He perceives man's natural inclinations and impulses as one means of expression which, if not associated with other means such as social conventions, does not afford the person any feeling of being free.

Tolstoy's concept of freedom decreases with knowledge because he assumes that the more man is aware of what he might do, the more he tends to be aware of what it would be correct for him to do, and the more he would feel obligated to do that correct thing. At the same time, as is suggested by Aquinas, it is not clear that an uninhibited expression of natural impulses should be regarded as a state of freedom for man.

The Kantian view asserts that man is free when he does what is reasonable and right. Here man may be thought of as the slave of his impulses when he translates them directly into action. For example, if a person decided to break with tradition and conformity by driving his automobile through a red light and thereby colliding with a number of pedestrians and cars, it is likely that he would not be regarded as free, but controlled by his feelings and urges. This corresponds with the psychoanalytic position. Analysts do not advocate an undisciplined expression of impulses, nor would they consider such a discharge a manifestation of freedom. Freedom implies due allowance given to the requirements of reality; it is not license. Thus inherent to the concept of freedom is restraint. To be free, man has to have limits and self-control. To evidence free will, man has to pause and reflect. Accordingly, free will is not a random exercise in choosing among equally desirable alternatives, but very often is experienced as a deliberate selection *determined* by what we believe or know to be proper, reasonable, and correct.

Man's freedom is circumscribed still further by his physical structure. There are physical limitations that exist for all of us—maturing and aging processes, the speed with which we can run, the boundaries of sensitivity of our sense organs, the concepts we can grasp, and the bodily needs we must satisfy for survival. In addition to these are the habits we have acquired, the personality characteristics we display, and the values, purposes, and goals that guide us. Armed with this information about the person, would his behavior now seem so unpredictable?

Nevertheless, those who believe in free will can contend that these limitations, some of which men have accepted of their own free will, can be thought of as borders within which they continue to function freely. They insist that these curbs on what man can do and what he should do, although they allow a semblance of predictability and determinism in connection with human conduct, are not crucial in refuting the concept of free will. It is at this point that the determinists can bring in a final telling argument—unconscious motivation.

That unconscious wishes, prohibitions, injunctions, and impulses—variables that act to influence man without his awareness—perform in countless ways to distort his perceptions, affect his judgments and convictions, and compel his behavior has been so well documented and illustrated as to be beyond any reasonable doubt. Freud's pioneering investigations, since repeated time and again, have demonstrated the pervasiveness of unconscious motivation, not only in matters of great consequence and in apparently meaningless symptoms, but also in ordinary, easily overlooked accidents and mishaps: "All of these (slips of the tongue, forgetting of names, etc.) . . . were shown to be strictly determined and were revealed as an expression of the subject's suppressed intentions or as a result of a clash between two intentions one of which was permanently or temporarily unconscious" (Freud, 1959).

The construct of the unconscious has been highly profitable for the determinist position, for it has made explicable and predictable events that flew in the face of reason and that were dismissed as perverse and chance occurrences. Here were behaviors that the person could not explain. Here were acts that seemed to take place without his will and even against his will. But rather than being mere quirks, these "I don't know why I did that" and "I don't know what got into me" situations yielded to the assumption that they were determined and purposeful. Given this insight into human behavior, man no longer seemed so mysterious or so rational.

Show me an individual who claims to have exercised his free will, says the determinist, and I will show that no other choice was as probable. Show me a person who has freely made a complex decision, says the determinist, and I will show that he was also directed by forces unknown to him. Where, outside of phenomenological reality, does free will exist?

RESOLUTIONS OF THE CONTROVERSY

It is conceded by determinists that people in general have little question about their free will, and let us assume that our knowledge of this controversy has led us to the conviction that such freedom has no basis in reality. Does this mean that free will in every sense ceases to exist? Would it make the feeling that people have that they are free any the less significant to the determinist or to them? Are not other perceptions and beliefs, for example, pain, beauty, and prejudice, important and amenable to study despite their lack of objective reality? Could not people believe, or not believe, that they act freely, and could not determinists assume that humans act in predictable fashion, with both deriving profit from their separate assumptions?

There is little question in the scientific community about the value of determinism. By assuming that all events are determined, science has been led into profitable explorations of areas that might earlier have been shrugged off as inconsequential or inexplicable. By not assuming the existence of supernatural forces to account for the phenomena it studies, science has left man somewhat alone in nature, but, paradoxically, it has left scientists feeling more controlling than controlled.

Yet determinists recognize that their position about man's behavior is not obvious, and that they are often required to explain it to an audience that may be rather incredulous. Frequently, they find it necessary to argue that free will is an illusion that itself is quite simply determined (Immergluck, 1964). Turner (1966) has presented an example of this argument within the context of its use as a device to stimulate controversy in the classroom and on campus: "Our feelings of personal choice are strongest when we are so unaware of the stimuli causing our behavior that we have no alternative to conclude, incorrectly, that we ourselves were the source of the action. Since we are often ignorant of the stimuli guiding our behavior . . . we frequently have the illusion of free will."

This resolution of the controversy, that free will is a useful illusion, but an illusion nevertheless, has its counterpart among those who believe in free will; they analyze determinism and find that it is a profitable fabrication, but a fabrication nonetheless (Hartmann, 1961). The two major points made in support of this contention are usually the following:

1. We cannot state with absolute certainty that one event determines another, but can only, with varying degrees of confidence, attribute causality to events that appear to us to be regularly associated. Scientists cannot say what determines what. Instead, they describe a sequence of events. For example, it is not possible ever to say that smoking causes lung cancer; it can only be said that to a certain extent smoking and lung cancer are found together. Thus determinists cannot be completely sure of their predictions, and they must, in all honesty, qualify their statements of what may happen with considerations of probability.

2. There are no actual, immutable scienific laws but merely our records and constructions of what seem to be certain regularities in our observations. Accordingly, even in the most elegant and precise of our sciences, not determinism, but an amount of indeterminism exists. To quote Mabbott (1967): "No scientist will claim to say *why* any event happens; no scientist will ever claim to predict with certainty *that* it will happen. . . . all scientific prediction is based on observed statistical regularities and can never yield more than a probable result."

Yet now it is the turn of the determinists to counter. Granting that behavior cannot be analyzed into cause and effect relationships, and granting that it is not possible to state with perfect certainty that something will occur, still is it not true that what the individual will do in a given situation is completely determined by his personality and the circumstances? In other words, is not free will a bit of excess baggage that has no essential place in explaining human behavior? For it can be argued that free will is determined, that the choices that occur to a person are a function of his personality.

Furthermore, it has been pointed out by May (1969) that even if it were possible for a scientist to amass all the information about a person that would be needed to predict his behavior, the knowledge by the subject that this material has been accumulated and that predictions about his acts will be made introduces new elements into the system. The effects of these new elements could alter his system so that unpredicted behaviors would occur, at least for the first few times anyway.

It is the certitude about habit and compulsion and the room for error in scientific understanding that trouble many who have given serious consideration to the problem of free will and determinism. May's resolution is bittersweet and somewhat disappointing to those who favor closure, but it resonates with man's efforts to comprehend his existence—there are problems that have no solutions, and that yield to those who grapple with them, not answers, but deeper, richer appreciations of what is involved.

Yet is this issue insolvable? Or is this another instance of words creating a reality that does not actually exist? For example, it can be argued that before a person walks across a room, he has to cover half the distance; before he covers that half, he has to cover half its distance; and since there are an infinite number of half distances he has to traverse, he can never make it across the room. Another example: there is an infinity of time past and an infinity of time to come; and each day that goes by is added to the infinity of time past; but how can one infinity be larger than another?

Perhaps the controversy about free will and determinism is another illustration of how our words can confound us. To be sure, one problem in resolving it is that our understanding has grown, but the terms have remained the same. Scientists no longer believe that determinism in a strict sense exists, and still it is possible to find them using the word "determines" when they really mean "describes" or "is associated with." Would anyone quarrel with the notion that he can be described, that relationships in his behavior can be identified, and that his belief in free will is associated with certain events in his life?

Nor, as we noted earlier, do we use "free" in a strict sense when we apply it to human behavior. The simple discharge of impulses is not freedom with reference to man. Rather man is thought to be free when he exercises control over his impulses. When there is no proper restraint, authorities speak not of freedom, but of an "irresistible impulse" or compulsion. In speaking of human behavior that is free, people mean, in part, that it is reasonable; which means that it shows regard for the rewards and punishments that are associated with it, that is, it is "determined." So long as man remains a social being, he can never be completely free. Nor would people believe themselves to be free if their behavior were completely natural, impulsive, or unpredictable. To most persons, the exercise of free will, of choice, means to show due regard for reality, to do what is predictable to them, to insure that their behavior is determined.

Therefore, while it is possible to conclude from this line of reasoning that both free will and determinism do not exist, an equally legitimate conclusion is that neither has an independent existence and both are acquired concepts that are of importance in determining human behavior, whether the behavior be that of the scientist or the hippie.

From this it follows that it is fruitless to contend that a decision must be made as to whether to believe in free will or determinism. This is a needless dilemma. Consider that within the individual's own personal experiences they are not mutually exclusive categories. On the contrary, it is precisely under circumstances when people can see their behavior as determined that they can also perceive themselves giving expression to their wishes and values and meeting with reason the demands and opportunities presented to them by their external environment. For if they do not have some understanding of what influences their conduct, far from believing that they have acted freely, they either dismiss the act as inconsequential or experience bewilderment and concern.

Titchener, in 1902, described a similar formulation to the one being advanced here: ". . . we find Professor Wundt . . . referring the final settlement of the dispute between determinism and indeterminism to philosophy, but himself maintaining, as psychologist, the thesis that 'voluntary and involuntary' actions differ not as causeless and caused, but 'rather in the *character* of the causality' to which they are subject. We need not seek further. If we believe in the spontaneity of the mind, functionally regarded, we do so (as we did before) for extra-psychological reasons."

Thus whether scientists regard free will and determinism as frames of reference that they may adopt from time to time to help them comprehend their own behavior or that of others (Budd, 1959), or whether they consider them to be hypothetical constructs or intervening variables (Wolfensberger, 1961), they can investigate them as beliefs in order to assess their acquisition and their effects on those who subscribe to them. This would be a useful task, and it would attempt to explore questions such as the following:

Do people differ in the freedom they believe they exercise?

What are the antecedents and consequents of these beliefs?

Are they associated with certain personality disturbances, with certain levels of accomplishment, with certain personality characteristics?

Do these beliefs undergo modification during psychotherapy?

Are they of importance in predicting who will benefit from psychotherapy and who will not?

Are they significant variables for differentiating among therapies and therapists, and are they perceived by clients so as to influence their impressions of therapists?

Let us see what light can be shed on these matters.

RELEVANCE OF THE ISSUE TO PSYCHOTHERAPY

It may be recalled that in the previous chapter studies by Strupp (1958) and Sundland and Barker (1962) found differences in the attitudes of therapists toward the planning and control of the treatment process. In turn, these attitudes appear to be related to the degree in which therapists believe in determinism or unconscious motivation and in free will. Although it is true that many therapists subscribe to determinism, and free will too for that matter, there are differences in emphasis that are reflected in different theories and therapeutic approaches.

Moreover, while most psychotherapists are quite aware of the theoretical and philosophical differences that exist among them, there is little information available as to whether these distinctions are so readily apparent to their prospective clients. Further, it is not known if clients would respond to these differences with reactions similar to those of some therapists. To be specific, the emergence of behavior therapies within recent years has raised profound concerns for some therapists about the degree of control imposed and the violations of the client's human dignity and right to exercise choice. Yet there is no evidence to suggest that clients who are treated by behavior therapists share these concerns, and there is some evidence to indicate that, at least at first, the issue of free will and determinism is irrelevant to the impressions that people form of therapists.

In a study by the author a questionnaire was administered to 134 undergraduate students in introductory psychology. This questionnaire was designed to measure beliefs in free will, unconscious motivation, and determinism by explicit statements inquiring into these beliefs. As a group, the students professed an inclination to believe in all three. That this somewhat inconsistent finding was not simply owing to a tendency to agree with items was indicated by the fact that a belief in free will required disagreement with certain statements. Moreover, this inconsistency in beliefs would not be solely a peculiarity of students, for, as has already been noted, there are indications that it can be found among professionals as well.

After responding to the questionnaire, the students were asked to listen to three taped excerpts of psychotherapy interviews (Shapiro, 1964, pp. 55–56, 42–43, 63–64), the first conducted by a psychoanalyst, the second by a Rogerian therapist, and the third by a behavior therapist. After each selection, ratings were made of the therapist's understanding, respect, and helpfulness on a four-point scale, with high scores indicating more favorable ratings. Finally, the students were asked to select which of the three types of therapy they would prefer if they were going to be seen in treatment.

The tapes were introduced in the following manner:

I am going to play selections from three types of psychotherapy interviews. Each of these interviews is conducted by a therapist who is a recognized authority in his method of treatment. I would like you to pay particular attention to the therapist because I shall be asking you for your impressions of him. The first therapist you will hear is a psychoanalyst, Franz Alexander. Psychoanalysis emphasizes that symptoms are expressions of unconscious conflicts, and the analyst tries to tie together how we behave in the present with our wishes and feelings in the past. Unfortunately, the quality of this recording is not too good, but I think you will be able to understand much of what he says and get a feeling of the kind of therapist he is.

The second therapist is a Rogerian or client-centered therapist, Thomas Gordon. Rogerian therapy tries to help the person to see his feelings clearly, to evaluate his standards and aspirations, and to become more accepting of himself or self-satisfied. It believes that a major reason for psychological disorders is that people are dissatisfied by the difference between what they are and what they would like to be, and so it tries to bring about greater self-satisfaction.

The third therapist is a behavior therapist, Arnold Lazarus. Behavior therapists emphasize that psychological disorders are learned. They try to train the person to feel more relaxed in situations that were anxiety-arousing and to act more appropriately.

The results of this study were quite surprising. There was a highly significant difference in the preference expressed by students for behavior therapy, with 98 picking it, while only 20 picked Rogerian therapy and 16 chose psychoanalysis. This difference was also expressed in the mean ratings given the therapists on understanding (2.8, 2.4, and 3.6, respectively), on respect (2.8, 2.8, and 3.4), and on help (2.7, 2.0, and 3.7). Although it was clear that the behavior therapist was rated more favorably than the other two, the ratings had no apparent relationship to beliefs in free will, determinism, and unconscious motivation. Even among students who differed diametrically in their responses to the questionnaire items, there was agreement in their evaluations of the therapists. It seemed that the metasystems of psychotherapy were either irrelevant or not apparent to students from taped excerpts of therapy interviews.

It was decided to repeat the ratings of the therapists with the following refinements: (a) since the recording of the analyst was of poor quality, it was recorded over again with the author playing the role of Alexander and with a graduate student playing the role of the patient; and (b) a female graduate student who had no interest in the study was recruited to conduct its replication. Accordingly, the tapes were administered six months later to an evening class in introductory psychology composed of 90 students. The results were virtually the same as in the previous study: 64 students indicated a preference for behavior therapy, 18 for analysis, and 8 for Rogerian therapy.

Now it seemed to be appropriate to repeat the study but this time to make explicit the metasystems of the therapists in order to see whether they were relevant to the students. An introductory psychology class of 102 students took the questionnaire and then heard the tapes, which in this study were introduced as follows:

> The first therapist you will hear is Franz Alexander, a psychoanalyst. Unfortunately, the quality of the original recording was not too good, and so it was recorded over again with a student playing the client and with me playing Alexander. Although our acting leaves much to be desired, the words are exactly the same as those used by Alexander and his client, and so I think you will be able to get a feeling for the kind of therapist an analyst is. What the analyst tries to do is to help the client to understand the meaning of his dreams and to see how important the wishes and fears of his childhood are to him, even as an adult. He tries to get the client to see the very great significance of his early years as a child as an influence upon the problems he now faces.

> The second therapist is a Rogerian or client-centered therapist, Thomas Gordon. He is seeing a young woman and is trying to help her to understand her feelings more clearly. Rogerian therapists believe that people can be helped best by being given the freedom to make their own decisions and choices. The Rogerian therapist avoids telling his client what to think or do. Instead, he tries to help his client to feel free to decide for herself what she believes and wants.

> The third therapist is a behavior therapist, Arnold Lazarus. Behavior therapists believe that people learn to behave in maladjusted ways and that they can be trained to behave appropriately. A behavior therapist is not usually concerned about his client's childhood, hidden feelings and problems. He believes it is possible to change and to control a person's behavior by giving rewards and punishments. In this selection, Lazarus is trying to get his client to feel less afraid by feeling more relaxed. You'll notice that the behavior therapist does not worry about his client's freedom, but takes charge and directs the client in what to do.

These different introductions had a marked effect on the selection of therapies: 38 students picked Rogerian therapy, 37 behavior therapy, and 27 psychoanalysis. However, although there was a tendency for the analyst to be rated higher by those who scored high on a belief in unconscious motivation, there was no other appreciable effect on the ratings of the therapists, and there was no enhancement of the relationship between the ratings and the responses to the questionnaire. Thus the behavior therapist was still rated most favorably by virtually all the students, but the Rogerian therapy, with its emphasis upon the individual's freedom, appeared to become more attractive than it had been.

Take together, the findings of the studies indicate that beliefs in free will, determinism, and unconscious motivation are probably of little relevance to prospective clients in forming initial impressions of therapists. This does not necessarily mean that these beliefs are unimportant to clients, but it does suggest that in the beginning of the treatment situation, which it should be remembered is a help-seeking and help-giving one, that the therapist's convictions in these matters are less pertinent to his clients than some of his other attributes.

Moreover, the findings suggest that the techniques or manner by which therapists seek to implement or convey their beliefs in free will and determinism are not at first perceived by clients in the way intended. This was particularly true with Rogerian therapy, where a brief presentation of its rationale aided considerably in enhancing its appeal to the students. Accordingly, Rogerian therapists might be well advised to consider giving a short explanation of their philosophy of psychotherapy to those of their clients who are unfamiliar with it.

Another point of interest is the lack of relationship between beliefs and the ratings of the behavior therapist. It is quite possible that in this selection from the interview it appeared to the students that the behavior therapist provided ample opportunity to his client for the exercise of choice, even though a desensitization procedure impresses many professionals as very controlling. Further, it is possible that as treatment progresses these issues become more salient to clients than they are at the beginning. Whatever the explanation, it is certain that beliefs in free will and determinism are of considerable consequence to therapists, who appreciate and are sensitive to their implications for theory building and practice.

In some systems of psychotherapy, such as Rank's will therapy, Rogerian therapy, and existential analysis, central importance is ascribed to the freedom of the individual. For Rogers, it is the creation of the experience of freedom in treatment that allows personal growth to proceed. His ideal goal in psychotherapy is the "fully functioning person," one who feels free even though all his actions are determined. This contrasts with the "defensive person," one who feels constrained and unable to implement his choices (Rogers, 1961). While Rogers, as a psychologist-scientist assumes that he has no choice but to be deterministic, it is clear that he places great significance in the individual's having the feeling that he is free, even though this feeling may have no foundation in reality.

Rank sees the expression of individuality as a universal, core problem for man. How is one to assert one's own wishes, ideas, and choices; how is one to stand alone without feeling terrified? For each failure to express one's thoughts arouses guilt about self-betrayal, and each instance of acquiescence causes feelings of anxiety to mount as the possibility increases that one's own individuality will be lost irretrievably. The ideal solution is to conform when it is reasonable without feeling guilty, and to be independent, assertive, and expressive of one's own will without feeling afraid.

Similarly, to many existentialists the failures of men to exercise their free will is a failure in being human. They would argue that to deny that one has the option of exercising choice is a denial of one's humanity. And such failures and denials are not purchased without cost. Quite to the contrary, the cost to the individual is thought to be enormous. A total denial of free will would result, it is contended, in a dehumanized being, devoid of any feeling of responsibility for his actions and deprived of any zest or enthusiasm for life. This unhappy outcome would be pathological.

Within these therapies, and within society as a whole, value is placed upon the person who acts freely and in accordance with his own will, even though this may place him in conflict with traditions and social pressures. In Riesman's formulation of personality types, for example, the ideal is the autonomous type, which is defined as ". . . those who on the whole are capable of conforming to the behavioral norms of their society . . . but are free to choose whether to conform or not" (Riesman et al., 1955). While Rank said much the same thing as Riesman, Rank placed it within the context of a far broader generalization: "In the ceaseless struggle for liberation of self from the moral, social, aesthetic ideologies and the people who represent them, the individual goes through a disjunctive process of which I have regarded the process of birth as the prototype. . . . it is, broadly, the attempt of the individual to gain a freedom from dependence of any sort upon a state from which it has grown" (Rank, 1932). And as a final illustration we may quote Binswanger's gerundive phrasing of virtually the same basic idea: ". . . existential analysis holds to the fact that being human is not only a having-to-be but also a being-able-to-be and a being-allowed-to-be, a being secure in being as a whole" (Binswanger, 1958).

For those professionals who believe in free will, or some closely related spirit of it, the healthy person is thought to be spontaneous, creative, courageous, able to demonstrate initiative, flexible, and capable of setting off on his own in a new direction. His behavior would not be stereotyped.

It would have the capacity to surprise, to be somewhat unpredictable, and to be directed toward a variety of goals. Such a person is supposed to be vibrant with self-confidence, aglow with his own ideas, and sure both that his choices are his own and that he knows himself better than anyone else knows him.

In contrast to this ideally healthy person, who not only wishes to do things but goes ahead and does them, is the struggling neurotic, the unhappy and troubled individual who either feels unable to make choices of his own or who finds himself unable to act on certain decisions when he has reached them. He is dissatisfied with himself, concerned about his purpose in life, and unsure about his handling of people. He is the person the therapist sees.

These views of the ideal and disturbed individual are in the romantic tradition: ". . . a highly general attitude toward life and toward artistic expression that emphasizes freedom, spontaneity, the value of feeling and of fantasy" (English and English, 1958). And since the Romantic Movement flowered during the nineteenth century, it is there that we can find a pristine expression of its translation into psychotherapeutic prescriptions. To the therapists of an earlier day, psychological problems were due to some defect of will, some inability on the part of the troubled person to set his mind to thinking correctly. Perhaps the person was disappointed because he was too ambitious. Perhaps his self-esteem was constantly being wounded because his standards for himself were too high. Perhaps he had just not learned the proper habits or was having difficulty in breaking habits that were harmful. Whatever the problem, what was needed in each case was to restore the individual's self-confidence so that he would feel sufficiently inspired to embark on some desired course of action, and then to give him a fairly explicit and straightforward push in the right direction.

William James was probably the most famous proponent for this way of helping people. He had come to believe in its potency on the basis of its value in helping him with his own problems. During his young manhood, James had suffered for many years from intense, incapacitating periods of depression. After his graduation from medical school, he lapsed into a particularly severe period of mental anguish, and found his own personal salvation in the writings of the philosopher Charles Renouvier: "Man, according to Renouvier, has liberty as his fundamental characteristic: what a man believes is what he *chooses* to believe; a person may alter his beliefs by an exercise of his will" (Reisman, 1966). This proved to be a turning point in James' life, and he was convinced that he had succeeded in rescuing himself from a life of invalidism by the simple expedient of resolving to become active and happy.

James' own good fortune in straightening himself out through will power made it seem plausible to him that in many cases all one needed to do to feel better was to set one's mind to it. His theory of emotions was associated with this belief; and it led him to advocate that if one wished to experience a certain feeling, one should act in ways that normally accompany that affect. For example, if you wish to overcome a feeling of sadness, make an effort to smile; and if you can bring yourself to smile, you will find that you no longer feel as sad as you did before. Therefore, with boundless faith in the capacity of his fellow man to change and to exercise self-control, James offered what strike most professionals today as outrageously direct prescriptions for dealing with psychological ills: to overcome fears, act brave!

Admonitions to "snap out of it" and "keep your chin up" have little place in modern psychotherapeutic practice, although they enjoy popular use. Nevertheless, the belief in the strength of the individual and in his ability to deal with matters of which he is aware, a belief that serves as the basis for these admonitions, finds expression in systems of psychotherapy, particularly those of Rank, Rogers, and existential analysis. Moreover, the same belief exists in some of the most deterministic forms of psychotherapy, some methods of behavior therapy. The common thread that unites these strange bedfellows is the emphasis they give to conscious motivation; the feelings, perceptions, and beliefs of the present; and the capacity of the individual to cooperate in an effort to modify his attitudes and behavior. But since one group has a fondness for free will and the other, the behavior therapist, does not, they differ greatly in their goals and attitudes.

Behavior therapists usually have a specific and limited goal, the modification of definite symptoms or behaviors. They do not stress unconscious functioning, nor do they concern themselves with conflicts or attitudes that appear to be unrelated to the problem at hand. Since they take the "symptom" or bit of troublesome behavior at face value, they convey the impression to the client that the problem is manageable and not of major proportions. Since they consider themselves expert in modifying behavior, they assume a large burden of responsibility for bringing about the desired changes and thus seem to be confident and hopeful. Since their therapeutic efforts, despite their control and in contrast to their training of behaviors, require cooperation, they inform the client implicitly or explicitly that he has control over his actions and that what he does can make a difference in how he feels and acts.

Therapists who are influenced by the concept of free will generally have a broad and nonspecific goal. They aim to help the person to become more accepting of himself, and thus to experience greater freedom in expression and in dealing with problems. Since their objective is the promotion of a reasonable, pleasurable independence (not to be confused with a noisy, hostile rebelliousness), they emphasize respect for the individual as a unique being; and in matters of judgment regard the person, not themselves, as the final arbiter. Thus if interpretations are made, they are offered as tentative efforts to attain an understanding of what the person himself is just about to put into words; and if an interpretation is rejected, the rejection is seen not as resistance, but as a healthy expression of independence, as well as evidence of a poor interpretation.

An important task of these therapists is to assist the client to assume responsibility for making choices. This is accomplished both by making clear the range of possibilities and the feelings associated with them, and by the oftentimes difficult acceptance of a decision that the person experiences as his own. Some of these decisions may seem unwise to the therapist and some may be very threatening. Yet (and it should be noted that few issues in psychotherapy arouse as much disagreement as this one) the therapist after bringing forward what is relevant to arriving at a decision feels he must respect the choice that is made by the person who believes he is acting freely.

Now just as behavior therapists are in some agreement with those who believe in free will, so also are they in some agreement with psychoanalysts. Both are markedly deterministic in their orientation. Therefore despite the many differences in theory and technique that exist between them, they share beliefs that have a strong bearing on their practice of psychotherapy.

Each regards the therapist as an expert in understanding human behavior in general and the behavior of each client in particular. While individuals differ, and for a time the therapist himself may be baffled by a specific case, it is assumed that, almost without exception, the therapist's understanding of the client's motivation and troubling behaviors is superior to the understanding possessed by the client. That this should be so follows reasonably from several considerations: (a) Although few therapists would go so far as to label their clients as "stupid" (Dollard and Miller, 1950), they believe that these people are remarkably inept when it comes to coping with those problems that cause them to seek help, otherwise why would they have to seek help? (b) The therapist brings into the situation his ability to evaluate it objectively and with considerable sophistication. (c) The therapist's perceptions in this area, unlike those of the client, are not distorted by unconscious impulses and wishes. (d) As is well known, the client has little awareness of many of the relevant variables that influence his symptoms.

To be more specific, the behavior therapist believes he is an expert because his years of training have led him to an understanding of the applications of principles of learning that is superior to most. He does not concern himself with unconscious motivation, and proceeds on the assumption that he will see how far he can get the client to go without it. His desire is to be parsimonious in his explanatory concepts, and perhaps for that same reason he declines to burden himself with free will.

The psychoanalyst thinks of himself as an expert because of his lengthy training and study of psychoanalysis. His major concern is with unconscious motivation, and he is often troubled by the blithe disregard of behavior therapists of a variable whose importance is daily demonstrated in his work. Very frequently, he believes in free will and sees it operating in certain conflict-free areas of the ego. However, by the very fact that the client is pathological, there is clear evidence that internal forces are at work to disrupt proper functioning, hence to restrict freedom of choice and action. Thus he also sees his expertness brought about by the unfortunate circumstance that in matters of importance his clients are not really able to make use of free will. His task is "to restore their free will to his patients" (Erikson, 1967) by reducing the efforts of these hampering unconscious influences (Sager, 1959; Boigon, 1965).

Therefore, either because they do not believe in free will (mainly behavior therapists) or because they believe the client is unable to exercise his free will (psychoanalysts), deterministic therapists tend to play an active role, at least insofar as the actions or intended actions of their clients outside the treatment hour are concerned. In the behavior therapies, there is no question that the therapist does strive to control, manipulate, and order the situation to the client's advantage. However, since in psychoanalysis the role of the therapist is often described as "passive," the activity that we are trying to describe requires some amplification.

What is meant by "active" in this context is that the analytic therapist, at the beginning of treatment or during its course, indicates that not all decisions "freely" reached by the client can be accepted. As Wolberg (1967, p. 564) put it: "If you contemplate any significant alteration in your position or life situation, it is essential to talk it over with your therapist first, in order to make sure that you are not being influenced by temporary emotional feelings stirred up during treatment." In such ways, psychoanalysts assume far greater responsibility for their clients than those who place much value on the client's making his own decisions.

For the deterministic therapists, the immediate objective is not so much the expression of individuality and the acceptance of responsibility as it is the promotion of a kind of equilibrium so that the person can function effectively, that is, in keeping with the demands and requirements of reality. This aim of bringing about a relatively stable adjustment accounts for the use of terms such as "unbalanced," "disturbed," and "maladjusted" in describing their clients. The goal may be considered to have been attained by behavior therapists when there is a reduction or a modification of symptoms (Wolpe, 1958), but this is regarded as a modest and perhaps deceptive result by the analysts if there is no indication that the intrapsychic conflicts have been resolved: "Symptoms, however, are surface phenomena, the outward manifestations of some underlying condition of disorder" (White, 1964). Accordingly, the analyst's long-range goals are the reduction of unconscious turmoil and the promotion of a favorable balance of intrapsychic systems, thus allowing the individual to function freely.

This analysis suggests that therapists who are humanistic (existential therapists, Rogerians, and psychoanalysts) have a similar concept of the goal of treatment, to enable the person to feel free; both behavior therapists and analytic therapists see themselves as having the ultimate responsibility for the course of treatment; and both behavior therapists and those who see the free will of the client as denied but not impaired emphasize the importance of conscious motivation and the ability of the individual to cooperate in the treatment and effect changes in himself. Thus therapists differ among themselves in goals, anthropomeliorism, and the extent of responsibility that they believe they must assume for their clients. In turn, these differences are probably related to differences in the duration of treatment and to differences in free will-determinism, and the relative significance of conscious-unconscious motivation.

It also seems quite likely that these differences are not without their parallels among clients, that is, that some people believe strongly in the importance of their free will, their exercise of independent choice, and their capacity for change, while others may be more impressed by their inability to understand and to control themselves and desire mainly a feeling of tension relief or "peace of mind." The variable that appears to be emerging is somewhat akin to the internal-external control dimension that was discussed earlier. However, the items of the I-E scale seem to assess internal control versus no control (chance, fate, luck), while what is being discussed here is wanting to be in control versus feeling a need to be controlled. Put another way: to what extent does the person believe he is able to control his behavior and to what extent does he believe he needs to have his behavior controlled.

This variable appears to be related to dependency, which has been found to be associated with the length of time the client would remain in psychotherapy (Winder et al., 1962). That is, clients whose expressions of dependency are reinforced tend to stay in treatment longer that those whose expressions of dependency are ignored. However, within this context what would be expected to be found is that clients who wish to be controlled (dependent) are better served by therapists who believe they ought to be controlling, while clients who want to be controlled are better served by therapists who believe they ought not be controlling. It is a matter of matching on what is a highly important therapist-client variable.

It is also known that some clients believe in the significance of unconscious motivation, while others do not see it as personally relevant, and that there are therapists with compatible views. Therefore, given the possibility of treatment choice, it would be sensible to match clients who want to be controlled and who stress conscious motivation with behavior therapists; clients who emphasize unconscious motivation and who favor being controlled with psychoanalysts; and clients who favor conscious motivation and who resent being controlled with Rogerian or existential therapists.

In order to investigate the value and feasibility of matching on the variables of control and unconscious motivation, two relatively simple rating scales were devised by the author in the form of a questionnaire, called the D-U Scale (Direction—Unconscious motivation Scale). An answer sheet on which the person could indicate his agreement or disagreement with each item along a four-point scale accompanied the questionnaire, the description of which follows.

D-U Scale

The following items ask you to describe the kind of psychotherapist you would like and what you believe the work of the client should be. Check your agreement or disagreement with each item on the answer sheet. Do not mark on this paper.

1. The therapist should ask for his client's dreams and spend a significant part of the treatment in trying to interpret them.

2. The therapist should raise doubt about the client's explanations of the reasons for his behavior.

3. The therapist should direct the attention of the client to his childhood and to the relationships he had with his parents.

4. The therapist should challenge the wisdom of his client's decisions.

5. The therapist should bring the client to see how wishes and feelings of his childhood influence his behavior as an adult.

6. The therapist should give advice and suggestions to his client.

7. The therapist should try to reduce the client's symptoms without bothering to discover underlying reasons for their existence.

8. The therapist should help the client to change behavior by the proper administration of rewards and/or punishments.

9. The therapist should praise the client when he reports progress and often encourage him to change for the better.

10. The client should not make any important decisions without first discussing them with his therapist.

11. The client should recognize that reducing his symptoms is best accomplished by understanding the problems and conflicts of his childhood.

12. The client should remain in treatment until the therapist indicates the treatment has been thorough and complete.

13. The client should expect to wait a long time before experiencing any improvement in his symptoms.

14. The client should search for underlying reasons for his behavior.

15. The client should seek and accept the therapist's advice.

16. The client should forget about his childhood and concentrate on dealing with his current problems.

17. The client should not trouble himself about underlying feelings and problems.

18. The client should not expect to talk at length about personal problems.

These statements were presented to three clinical psychologists with the request that they categorize them into descriptions of psychoanalytic and behavioristic therapies. There was unanimous agreement that items 1, 2, 3, 5, 10, 11, 12, 13, and 14 described behaviors expected in psychoanalysis, while items 4, 6, 7, 8, 9, 15, 16, 17, and 18 were descriptive of behavior therapy; the first group of items made up the scores of the U scale, and the second group became the D scale. It was hypothesized that:

1. High scores on U are associated with preferences for psychoanalytic therapy.

2. High scores on D are associated with preferences for behavior therapy.

3. Low scores on D and low scores on U are associated with preferences for Rogerian therapy.

High scores on D and high scores on U indicate some problem in responding to the questionnaire since several of the items, for example, 11 and 16, are contradictory when both are answered affirmatively.

The procedure in this study was similar to that reported in the study about free will (see page 106). A group of 26 graduate students taking courses in clinical psychology and a group of 74 women attending a lecture series in continuing education answered the questionnaire; they then rated a psychoanalyst, a Rogerian therapist, and a behavior therapist as to understanding, respect, and helpfulness. These ratings were based on their impressions of taped excerpts of treatment interviews. Finally, they indicated which of the three types of therapy they would prefer if they were being seen in treatment.

In general, the results supported the hypotheses. Within the female sample, those who scored high on D, when compared with those who scored low, selected behavior therapy more frequently; while those who scored high on U rated the psychoanalyst more favorably than those who scored low. Within group comparisons were not possible in the graduate sample because of the homogeneity of responses and small number of students. However, it was possible to compare the differences between the two groups; they were statistically significant on all measures (see Table 1).

Table 1. Comparaison Between Graduate Student and Female Samples.

Sample	Mean scores and ratings[a]				
	D	U	Analyst	Rogerian	Behavior therapist
Female (N = 74)	19	25	9(27)	8(20)	10(27)
Student (N = 26)	21	22	8(5)	9(16)	9(5)

[a] Numbers in parentheses indicate number in sample who indicated preference for that form of treatment.

As a group, the students scored higher on D and lower on U than the female sample; also they indicated a preference for Rogerian therapy, which was the least preferred among the women. The items that distinguished between the two groups had to do with the importance of childhood (the women seemed to believe it necessary to take childhood events into account, while the students did not) and a behaviorist description of the role of the therapist (despite their Rogerian preference, the students could conceive of the therapist dispensing rewards and punishments, while the women disagreed with this role).

There are two points worthy of special mention. The first is that in discussing these findings with the graduate students, they indicated that their preferences were based primarily on their understanding of the metasystems of the different forms of psychotherapy. Their responses to the questionnaire were a professional matter, but their preferences were personal, at least to their way of thinking. Presumably, in the female sample personal considerations were of greater influence, both on the questionnaire and the evaluations of therapists, and these personal considerations may have included such irrelevant variables as the quality of the therapist's voice.

The second point is that in both samples the range of scores on the scales was limited. What the scores would be in a sample of patients or clients is a matter for conjecture and investigation. However, it is of great interest to note that the responses to the items agree with the findings of Orlinsky and Howard (1967). They asked 60 female patients who were being seen in outpatient psychotherapy to describe what they thought of as "a good therapy hour." The women described a session which was "psychoanalytic in content and experiential in manner," that is, a session in which the wishes and feelings of childhood were discussed and the therapist seemed to be a warm, friendly, giving human being. Although Orlinsky and Howard supposed that their results were restricted to a patient population experienced in psychotherapy, their "good therapy hour" was quite similar to the role descriptions given by the group of "naive" women on the D-U Scale.

To determine what effect the taped excerpts of the psychotherapy interviews had on the selection of type of treatment preferred, the D-U Scale was administered to a class of introductory psychology students attending summer school. After they had completed the questionnaire, they were given the following instructions.

As you know, psychotherapy is the use of psychological measures to treat psychological disorders. Usually a client is seen in psychotherapy at least once a week for a period of perhaps several months. Probably all of you when you think of psychotherapy, think of a particular form. However, there are many kinds of psychotherapy, and I would like your cooperation in telling me the kind of psychotherapist you would like. I am going to read you descriptions of three kinds of therapists, and then I want you to tell me the one kind you would prefer if you were going to be seen in psychotherapy.

The first type of therapist is a psychoanalyst. What the analyst tries to do is to help the client to understand the meaning of his dreams and to see how important the wishes and fears of his childhood are to him, even as an adult. He tries to get the client to see the very great significance of his early years as a child as an influence upon the problems he now faces.

The second type of therapist is a Rogerian or client-centered therapist. Rogerian therapists believe that people can be helped best by being given the freedom to make their own decisions and choices. The Rogerian therapist avoids telling his client what to think or do. Instead, he tries to help his client to feel free to decide for himself or herself what he or she believes and wants.

The third type of therapist is a behavior therapist. Behavior therapists believe that people learn to behave in maladjusted ways and that they can be trained to behave appropriately. A behavior therapist is not usually concerned about his client's childhood, free will, or hidden problems. He believes it is possible to change and to control a person's behavior by giving rewards and punishments, and so he usually takes charge and directs his client in what to do.

Now, if you were going to be seen in therapy, would you prefer a psychoanalyst, Rogerian therapist, or behavior therapist?

It will be recalled that after similar instructions were given and students heard the tapes, 38 picked Rogerian therapy, 37 behavior therapy, and 27 psychoanalysis. Under this condition, where a group of students did not hear the voices of the therapists, 33 picked psychoanalysis, 21 Rogerian therapy, and only 5 selected behavior therapy. The differences in choices between these two samples was significant ($\chi^2 = 9.53$; $p < .05$). This suggests that the recordings had an influence on the selections, and that this influence was most pronounced in the case of the behavior therapist. Evidently, actually hearing the behavior therapist did much to increase the attractiveness of his method of treatment. Quite possibly, the rationale for behavior therapy, unlike that of Rogerian therapy, is not an especial asset in attracting college students to seek it.

Also worthy of note is that in accord with expectations the students who selected psychoanalysis had a higher mean score on U than those who picked Rogerian therapy (26 versus 24; $t = 2.00$; $p < .05$); the mean scores on D were 21 for both groups. These findings and the results of the other studies previously considered suggest: (a) that there are differences among clients in the way they conceive of their role and the role of the therapist; (b) that these role concepts are related to preferences that clients may have about the type of treatment they receive and the impressions they initially form of therapists; and (c) that at times there are apt to be discrepancies between the ways therapists and clients view their roles.

It is reasonable to suppose that an as yet undetermined proportion of clients make an active attempt to match themselves with therapists they believe will be congenial. Probably this happens more frequently among a sophisticated and relatively wealthy clientele that has the opportunity to pick and choose among therapists. However, even among the less well-to-do this matching surely does go on. It may partially explain why so many clients break off from what starts out to be long term psychotherapy after about five interviews, and why they may stop with one therapist only to turn up immediately thereafter to seek the help of someone else.

As matters now stand, when the effects of psychotherapy are evaluated, it is done on the basis of results with a virtually haphazard matching of therapists and clients. Yet each day there is matching, whether therapists do anything about it or not. The decision is not whether there should be matching, but rather how aware and involved therapists wish to be in the need for clients to find an appropriate match. The client's and therapist's beliefs about their roles is one area that has not received too much consideration as a means for matching and possibly enhancing the effectiveness of psychotherapy. Such consideration is overdue.

CONCLUSIONS

Both free will and determinism exist as beliefs of people about human behavior. Both have value in influencing human conduct, and both are expressed in the convictions and practices of psychotherapists. Examined more closely, the free will-determinism variable in psychotherapy can be conceived of as two variables, conscious-unconscious motivation and the degree of control that the therapist exercises over the client in order to modify behavior. These in turn can be translated into therapist and client beliefs about their roles. The matching of therapist and client on these variables is probably important to the efficiency and effectiveness of psychotherapy, and one means for assessing the variables, the D-U Scale, has been described in order to demonstrate the feasibility of further study and investigation in this area.

CHAPTER 6

The Definition of Psychotherapy

The ancients who desired to illustrate illustrious virtue throughout the empire, first ordered well their own states. Wishing to order well their own states, they first regulated their families. Wishing to regulate their families, they first cultivated their own persons. Wishing to cultivate their persons, they first rectified their hearts. Wishing to rectify their hearts, they first sought to be sincere in their thoughts. Wishing to be sincere in their thoughts, they extended their knowledge to the utmost; and this extension of knowledge lay in the investigation of things.

Confucius

Psychotherapy has been defined as the communication of person-related understanding, respect, and a wish to be of help. This definition was arrived at by a scrutiny of variables found in representative forms of psychotherapy. First, a sample of definitions of this treatment method that had been offered by professionals of different orientations and disciplines was considered; these definitions were found to fall short of one or more standards, in that they were lacking in recognizability, precision, or independence from the goals of treatment. Then the setting in which therapy takes place, its duration, frequency, and participants were examined; variability and ingenuity were much in evidence, but practices that were derived from or supported by controlled empirical study were rare. Next, the participants were given a closer look and it was seen that the therapist and the client could vary in number and characteristics. The professional therapist, in particular, was observed to be subject to a wide range of changes. Conceivably, he could be eliminated completely from psychotherapy. He could hold widely different views about the nature of man. His skills and personal qualities did not seem to be definitive. In what way, it was wondered, are therapists of almost opposite styles the same? How is the persuasive, probing, controlling therapist similar to the accepting, reflecting, unobtrusive one? It was concluded that what is common among the various forms of therapy and therapists is a striving to communicate to clients their understanding of them and their problems, their respect, and their wish to be of help.

The implications of this definition will now be made explicit so as to enable an informed judgment to be made of its merits.

DISCUSSION OF THE TERMS OF THE DEFINITION

"Communication" refers to the transmission of a message. There is no specific instrument for sending the message—a deliberate omission to allow for whatever means may be attempted or employed. The professional psychotherapist is one means that has been used widely, and it may be that in the great majority of cases the therapist is the most efficient and effective device for conveying psychotherapy. However, the definition implicitly regards the therapist as only one medium or delivery system among many. Other media that have already been mentioned are motion pictures, tape recordings, and nonprofessionals, including the person himself. The reason for including the last item in the series is to state what is widely known, but what often goes unmentioned, that it is possible for the individual to reflect upon his beliefs, feelings, and behavior and to communicate to himself understanding of himself, respect, and a wish to be of help, that is, to provide himself with psychotherapy.

Further it should be made clear that the communication can be of any kind. Immediately, one thinks of words, written or spoken, but inflections and tones are also implied for they frequently are of greater importance in expressing meaning than the bare content of what is said. Moreover, while words are probably the major vehicle for communication at this time, there is room for actions and all the other nonverbal senders of messages to be included: facial expressions—from which people may be able to judge reliably the dimensions of attention-rejection, pleasantness-unpleasantness, and sleep-tension (Morgan, 1961); postures, gestures, positions of hands and feet; whatever cues are employed harmoniously, or sometimes not so harmoniously, with what a person may be trying to communicate at the moment. Accordingly, communication refers to any device or any means that people can have at their disposal for the transmission of messages. Although this medium today is usually a trained therapist who relies on speech to convey his thoughts to his clients, the definition does not preclude the possibility that at some future date communication may be largely mechanical and nonverbal.

Moreover, while the importance of the medium of transmission is recognized, and while it is believed that this medium has stimulus or message value, it is nevertheless asserted that psychotherapy is not the medium (therapist). Psychotherapy is the message, and the structure of the psycho-therapeutic message that every system seeks to send is: I understand you. I respect you. I wish to help you. Now, let us look at each of these central terms.

"Person-related understanding" refers to an attempt to comprehend the client's feelings, thoughts, actions, behavior. This attempt may or may not be empathic, and it may or may not be successful. In other words, the communicator may, from the frame of reference of someone else, have failed to grasp the meaning of what the client has said or done. He may have failed to see the unconscious implications, or to respond empathically. Even within the same theoretical orientation professionals may disagree among themselves as to whether there has been accurate understanding, or they may agree about the meaning and find that the client feels misunderstood. Regardless of these potential sources of disagreement, it is proposed that the communication be considered to be part of psychotherapy when it can be agreed that an attempt to understand the person has been made. This agreement is a necessary research strategy in order to enable an unbiased investigation of the effectiveness of different types of understanding.

For some therapists, understanding in psychotherapy has been construed narrowly as referring only to "empathic understanding," an effort to comprehend the person's immediate perceptions, feelings, and beliefs. To many professionals, such an understanding has at times been superficial and inappropriate to the significance of the client's remarks. Yet to those therapists who favor responding empathically, any other form of understanding is undesirable and an imposition of the therapist's will on the client. It seems quite possible that under some circumstances empathic understanding would be most effective, while under other circumstances another type of understanding would be appropriate. Accordingly, since it has not been demonstrated that one form of understanding is in all cases more therapeutic than another, it is best that in this integrative definition understanding be understood broadly, that it include an expert analysis or statement of explanation about the client's problem or course of action (expository understanding); as well as statements that relate the client's message to the past or to seemingly unrelated situations (interpretative understanding); as well as comments that acknowledge receipt of the client's communication (responsive understanding); as well as requests for clarification and information (interrogative understanding). To illustrate:

CLIENT: I suppose I really should have done something different.
THERAPIST   1:   You regret what you did (empathic understanding).

THERAPIST 2:   What do you suppose held you back? (interrogative).

THERAPIST 3:   Yet this seems to be the way you usually deal with these situations (interpretative).

THERAPIST 4:   You seem to be blaming yourself for a situation over which no one has any control (expository).

THERAPIST 5:   You'd like to have done it differently (empathic).

THERAPIST 6:   What did you want to do? (interrogative).

THERAPIST 7:   You've always found it hard to take a firm stand with people who remind you of your mother (interpretative).

THERAPIST 8:   Let's try to figure out what other things you might have done by going over the situation in more detail (expository).

For now all of the above therapist remarks would be thought of as types of person-related understanding, although research might demonstrate that some of these types are not effective and thus enable the definition to be refined.

"Respect" in this context has nothing to do with the deference accorded superiors in rank, socioeconomic status, prestige, or power. Rather it refers to the regard that the therapist has for the client as an individual, as a person. The feelings of the client, his sensitivity as a fellow human being are taken into account by the therapist, or whoever is responsible for the treatment. In "therapist"-client interactions, the "therapist" avoids rudeness, insults, smugness, contempt, ridicule, and anything that might be damaging to the client. Every effort is made to treat the client with proper courtesy and consideration.

Further, "respect" in this context implies that the therapist is intellectually aware that each client differs to some extent from every other client. There is a sobering recognition of dealing with a unique person, whose experiences and background are unlike those of anyone else, and about whom inevitably there will be missing pieces of information. So, the therapist recognizes that his understanding of this particular person is now, and must continue to be, incomplete, and that his ability to be of help is limited. No matter how expert he may be or how earnestly he may try, his efforts alone cannot guarantee the modification of beliefs or behavior. He cannot order or compel change. The cooperation of his client is essential. Therefore, it would not be incorrect to say that a nurturing background for respect as it is here being expounded is the therapist's humility.

In addition, respect indicates that the therapist recognizes, or acts as if he believes, that his client is able to make certain decisions for himself and is able to exercise some personal responsibility. Although professionals differ among themselves as to how much choice and responsibility, if any at all, is actually exercised by anyone, they all would probably agree that they usually convey the impression to their clients of the existence of some individual initiative and freedom, of some client responsibility for participation in the treatment.

While again this may seem all too obvious, for the sake of completeness it should be added that the therapist respects his client's right to have opinions and beliefs that differ from his own. No attempt is made to alter or explore or question the reasons for these convictions, unless the client himself chooses to discuss them. For example, the therapist does not try to convert his client to his religion or political party, nor does he challenge prejudices or biases, unless it is germane to do so, even though he may strongly disagree with them.

Finally we come to the last term in the definition, "a wish to be of help." This would seem, under ordinary circumstances, to be rather clear-cut and self-evident both to the therapist and to the client. Quite simply, the therapist wants to be of assistance in treating the individual's personal problems. That this should be his intention may be required by law. Certainly it is assumed by the public that the therapist, as a member of a profession that provides services, wishes to be of help, even before there has been any contact with him and even should he never make any avowed declaration that such is his aim. Therefore, at least at first a wish to be of help is assumed; it is taken for granted.

However, it is not too long before this wish to be of help may not be so obvious to the client. Demands may be made by him that appear reasonable, but that are thought unreasonable by the therapist. Rules and regulations, "limits," are imposed by the therapist that are necessary and sensible to him, but that may seem arbitrary and thoughtless to the client. Appointments have to end at a certain time for the orderly functioning of the office, despite the client's wish that they be extended. A meeting is suddenly cancelled because the therapist is ill, even though the therapist knows that this is very disappointing to the client. There are holidays, vacations, and trips to conventions, perfectly justified absences that occur in the lives of all professionals, which by any reasonable standard are entitled to occur, and which nevertheless many clients resent. These interruptions and limitations communicate the needs of the therapist and ask for the understanding of the client. The implications of the fact that this understanding may not be available should be considered. It would be prudent to recognize that as the treatment progresses special pains may have to be taken by the therapist to communicate explicitly his wish to be of help, and particularly would this objective need to be reaffirmed when there seems to the client to be evidence to the contrary.

IMPLICATIONS OF THE DEFINITION FOR RESEARCH

It is clear that the meanings intended for person-related understanding, respect, and a wish to be of help are broad and full. For the present it is best that these terms retain their rich and familiar meanings and that they not be construed as bound to a specific theoretical usage. Also, they should be thought of as essential qualities of psychotherapy, but for purposes of research, as relatively independent of one another. By so doing, it becomes possible to investigate the consequences of such situations as the following:

1. A person does not communicate person-related understanding and respect, but does communicate a wish to be of help.
2. A person does not communicate person-related understanding and a wish to be of help, but does communicate respect.
3. A person does not communicate respect and a wish to be of help, but does communicate person-related understanding.
4. A person does not communicate person-related understanding, but does communicate respect and a wish to be of help.
5. A person does not communicate respect, but does communicate person-related understanding and a wish to be of help.
6. A person does not communicate a wish to be of help, but does communicate person-related understanding and respect.
7. A person does not communicate person-related understanding, respect, or a wish to be of help.
8. A person communicates person-related understanding, respect, and a wish to be of help.

Then the differential effects, if any, that these conditions have on others can be explored. It would be expected that the most therapeutic or favorably regarded condition would be 8.

Another research area that is of great interest is the assessment of the communications of different systems of psychotherapy, that is, an analysis of the frequencies or proportions of communications of person-related understanding, respect, and a wish to be of help in one system as compared with another.

But it is possible to argue that these questions are premature. For it is of little ultimate consequence to study systems of psychotherapy until

of the method or of the clients themselves. Such studies would lead to the identification of those clients who are most helped by the communication of person-related understanding, respect, and a wish to be of help. Thus the definition allows for a conception of psychotherapy that would enable its antecedents and consequents to be traced with a minimum of prejudgments.

FURTHER IMPLICATIONS OF THE DEFINITION

The definition of psychotherapy that has been offered concentrates on the message and not the sender of that message. At first, the implications of this may be unsettling, for it suggests that, conceivably, psychotherapy could be conducted by anyone anywhere—in the beauty shop, the grocery store, and the family kitchen. All that would be required is that something or someone be communicating to someone else that he is understood, respected, and thought worthy of being helped. (That, presumably, is the impact of the psychotherapy message: he understands, respects, and wishes to help me.) Is it intended that the definition be taken to imply such a possibility? The answer: yes.

But this immediately compels the distinction to be made between the professional and nonprofessional use of this form of communication. If psychotherapy could be so pervasive, why does the professional who offers psychotherapy believe it to be so out of the ordinary and a skill that must be acquired by years of considerable training? This question might better be answered by being reformulated into two questions. One, is professional psychotherapy unusual? Two, could psychotherapy be pervasive?

The answer to the first question is that, yes, unfortunately psychotherapy is not usually found in human interactions. Each day in living their lives, people encounter people, and from one another each would probably like to receive understanding, respect, and a wish to be helpful. But it is not too often that anyone has the pleasant experience of receiving this kind of message from others. The problem is that so many people want understanding, respect, and help for themselves, while too few people realize that this is also desired by others and are willing to give it.

So what an individual is apt to find in ordinary social situations is that each person presents his beliefs, feelings, and ideas and wants them to be understood, but in his preoccupation with his own need to communicate he ignores or minimizes the significance of another person's emotions and thoughts. Respect is likely to be given, but as a function of social roles. For example, a salesclerk will probably give his customers respect, but even under such prescribed circumstances it comes as somewhat of a pleasant surprise to receive it. A wish to be helpful may be more common. Yet when it is not accompanied by respect, it is apt to be perceived negatively as paternalism, interference, or meddlesomeness.

Understanding without respect or a wish to be helpful would probably suggest cold indifference, a callous disregard for feelings. Respect alone would seem to describe a servile person. The various other combinations suggest that an understanding person who wishes to be helpful but who does not give respect may be regarded as arrogant, smug, and contemptuous; that the person who gives respect and wishes to be helpful but who is not understanding is perhaps perceived as well-meaning, though eventually ineffectual and irritating; and that the person who gives respect and who is understanding but who does not communicate a wish to be of help is one who is finally viewed as impudent and withholding. All three parts of the message would be needed for the message to be regarded as psychotherapy by an independent judge, though the person to whom the message is sent may perceive it as complete even when it is not.

In brief contacts it is quite possible that the person assumes certain aspects of the message even when they are not transmitted. For example: when a patient sees a physician and has medication prescribed, he assumes that the physician understands his ailment, but the physician may not be certain of the diagnosis. When a waitress takes an order, so long as she is not rude or insulting, the diners assume that she respects them. When students talk to a teacher and tell him of their problems in learning his subject, they assume that he wishes to be of help to them. Accordingly, there may not be understanding, respect, or a wish to be of help, but the person's assumptions and expectations may fill in what is lacking and transform an ordinary communication into psychotherapy for him.

It would seem reasonable to suppose, then, that in an individual's social contacts he may encounter someone who does communicate person-related understanding, respect, and a wish to be of help, or who seems to offer such a communication. These communications would be psychotherapy, and an estimate of their occurrence outside of the professional offering of psychotherapy may be taken as an index of the psychological climate of a particular place or setting, the primary preventive aspects of a given locale, and a basis for predicting the incidence of "spontaneous" remissions.

However, the usual pattern is to interact with others who do not communicate person-related understanding, respect, and a wish to be of help, and such communications are seldom expected in our customary interactions. In contrast, most people assume that professional therapists will transmit this message. After all, that is their job. They have been trained for that purpose, and their training has included not only a cultivation of their ability to communicate in that way, but also the development of their capacity to comprehend the reasons for nuances of behavior. Their understanding is probably more subtle, sophisticated, and accurate than the understanding of most nonprofessionals. Yet even where the words of the therapist are no different from the words that the client might hear elsewhere, they would be perceived with the weight ascribed to the pronouncements of an authority. Therefore, it is to be expected that the communications of the professional therapist will more frequently be psychotherapy and that they will more often be perceived as psychotherapy than the communications of others.

Further, unlike others the client may meet, the psychotherapist offers the communication of person-related understanding, respect, and a wish to be of help consistently, and makes no personal demands of his own. From appointment to appointment, week after week, and not unusually year after year, he sends these messages to his client, without requiring that he himself be understood, respected, and helped. This is quite unlike the customary social exchange, where even when a person feels that he has been heard and understood he soon experiences the demand to listen and to be sympathetic to someone else. Thus the communications of the therapist are more frequently, consistently, and uniformly psychotherapy than where psychotherapy is found to occur naturally.

Still, there is no reason why the communication of person-related understanding, respect, and a wish to be of help should be confined to the office of the psychotherapist, and many reasons why it should not be so restricted. People can be encouraged to try to understand things from the other person's point of view. They can be urged to try to be helpful to their fellow man and to treat him with respect, and as we read these words it should be painfully obvious to us all that people have been exhorted to behave in just these ways for thousands of years. That they do not, that they find it so difficult, is not only a measure of the strength of their own needs, but also an indication of the importance of these qualities in human behavior.

Each person has it in his ability to make use of psychotherapy. He can in his day-to-day living communicate his understanding of what another person is saying and feeling, his respect, and his wish to be of help. It is highly probable that there is much to be gained by the practice of such communications, both for the senders and receivers of the message. Is there anything really to be lost?

CONCLUSIONS

Psychotherapy is not everything that is psychotherapeutic. It is not a relationship, nor does it depend for its existence upon the operations of professionals. Psychotherapy is a message. More precisely, psychotherapy is the communication of person-related understanding, respect, and a wish to be of help. This communication may be found in any interpersonal situation. However, the probability of its occurrence is maximized in professionally conducted psychotherapy where a deliberate effort is made to transmit messages of this kind consistently and in an integrated fashion by a person trained specifically for that purpose.

Yet the therapist should be regarded as only one means of communication and as a person of considerable variety. Although many questions are in need of further study, there has been enough research to compel the conclusion that there is no single kind of "good" therapist, but rather that there is an appropriate therapist for a particular client. Accordingly, compatible matching of therapist and client appears to be a significant means for enhancing the beneficial effects of psychotherapy. For the therapist's credibility and acceptability depend not only on his skill and efforts, but also on what his clients want and expect.

The definition of psychotherapy that has been formulated provides a means for identifying this method of treatment in a way that is recognizable, precise, and independent of its goals or effects. At the same time it suggests that psychotherapy as a form of communication can exist in any human interaction when one person conveys to another his understanding of that person, his respect, and his wish to be of help.

References

Ablesser, H. "Role-reversal" in a group-psychotherapy session. *Group Psychotherapy*, **15**: 321–325, 1962.

Abramson, H., ed. *The Use of LSD in Psychotherapy and Alcoholism.* New York: Bobbs-Merrill, 1967.

Ackerman, N., ed. *Exploring the Base for Family Therapy.* New York: Family Service Association of America, 1961.

Adler, A. *What Life Should Mean to You.* Boston: Little, Brown and Co., 1931.

Aldrich, C. K. Styles of intervention. *Psychiatry and Social Science Review,* **1** (11): 22–26, 1967.

Alexander, F., French, T. M., et al. *Psychoanalytic Therapy.* New York: Ronald, 1946.

Allen, F. H. *Psychotherapy with Children.* New York: W. W. Norton, 1942.

American Psychiatric Association *A Psychiatric Glossary.* New York: APA New York Publications Office, 1964.

American Psychological Association Committee on Legislation. *New York State Psychologist,* **19** (2): 1, 1967.

Angyal, A. *Neurosis and Treatment.* New York: Wiley, 1965.

Ansbacher, H. L., and Ansbacher, Rowena R. *The Individual Psychology of Alfred Adler.* New York: Basic Books, 1956.

Arnhoff, F. N. Reassessment of the trilogy: need, supply, and demand. *American Psychologist,* **23**: 312–316, 1968.

Auld, F., Jr., and White, Alice M. Sequential dependencies in psychotherapy. *Journal of Abnormal and Social Psychology,* **58**: 100–104, 1959.

Ayllon, T., and Haughton, E. Modification of symptomatic verbal behavior of mental patients. *Behavior Research and Therapy,* **2**: 87–97, 1964.

Bach, G. R. A theory of intimate aggression. *Psychological Reports,* **12**: 449–450, 1963.

Barnhart, C. L., ed. *The American College Dictionary.* New York: Harper, 1951.

Berelson, B., and Steiner, G. A. *Human Behavior.* New York: Harcourt, Brace, and World, 1964.

Bergin, A. E. The effects of psychotherapy: negative results revisited. *Journal of Counseling Psychology,* **10**: 244–250, 1963.

Bergin, A. E. Some implications of psychotherapy research for therapeutic practice. *Journal of Abnormal Psychology,* **71**: 235–246, 1966.

Berzins, J. I., Friedman, W. H., and Seidman, E. Relationship of the A-B variable to patient symptomatology and psychotherapy expectancies. *Journal of Abnormal Psychology,* **74**: 119–125, 1969.

Betz, Barbara J. Experiences in research in psychotherapy with schizophrenic patients. In Strupp, H. H., and Luborsky, L., eds. *Research in Psychotherapy.* Washington, D. C.: American Psychological Association, 1962.

Betz, Barbara J. Studies of the therapist's role in the treatment of the schizophrenic patient. *American Journal of Psychiatry,* **123**: 963–971, 1967.

Bindrim, P. A report on a nude marathon. In *Readings in Clinical Psychology Today.* Del Mar, California: CRM Books, 1970.

Binswanger, L. The case of Ellen West. In May, R., Angel, E., and Ellenberger, H. F., eds. *Existence.* New York: Basic Books, 1958.

Blau, T. H. An elephant's faithful 100%. *American Psychologist,* **21**: 1077, 1966.

Boigon, M. What leads to basic change in psychoanalytic therapy? A round-table discussion. *American Journal of Psychoanalysis,* **25**: 129–141, 1965.

Bowlby, J. *Maternal Care and Mental Health.* Geneva: World Health Organization, 1951.

* Brammer, L. M., and Shostrom, E. L. *Therapeutic Psychology: Fundamentals of Counseling and Psychotherapy.* Englewood Cliffs, N. J.: Prentice-Hall, 1960.

Brayfield, A. W. Human resources development. *American Psychologist,* **23**: 479, 482, 1968.

Budd, W. C. Free will versus determinism. *American Psychologist,* **12**: 49–50, 1959.

Butler, J. M., and Haigh, G. V. Changes in the relation between self-concepts and ideal concepts consequent upon client-centered counseling. In Rogers, C. R., and Dymond, Rosalind, F., eds. *Psychotherapy and Personality Change.* Chicago: University of Chicago Press, 1954.

Carkhuff, R. R., and Pierce, R. Differential effects of therapist race and social class upon patient depth of self-exploration in the initial clinical interview. *Journal of Consulting Psychology,* **31**: 632–634, 1967.

Carson, R. C., and Heine, R. W. Similarity and success in therapeutic dyads. *Journal of Consulting Psychology,* **26**: 38–43, 1962.

Catanzaro, R. J. Tape-a-drama in treating alcoholics. *Quarterly Journal of Studies on Alcohol,* **28**: 138–140, 1967.

Cautela, J. R. Covert sensitization. *Psychological Reports,* **20**: 459–468, 1967.

Chace, Marian. Dance as an adjunctive therapy with hospitalized mental patients. *Bulletin of the Menninger Clinic,* **17**: 219–225, 1953.

Colby, K. M., Watt, J. B., and Gilbert, J. P. A computer method of psychotherapy: Preliminary communication. *Journal of Nervous and Mental Disease,* **142** (2), 1966.

Corey, D. Q. The use of a reverse format in now psychotherapy. *Psychoanalytic Review,* **53**: 107–126, 1966.

Cornelison, F. S., Jr. Learning about behavior: a new technique: Self-Image Experience. *Mental Hygiene,* **50**: 584–587, 1966.

Corsini, R. J. The "behind your back" technique in group psychotherapy and psychodrama. *Group Psychotherapy,* **6**: 102–109, 1953.

Corsini, R. J. *Methods of Group Psychotherapy.* New York: McGraw-Hill, 1957.

Cowen, E. L., Zax, M., Izzo, L. D., and Trost, Mary A. Prevention of emotional disorders in the school setting: A further investigation. *Journal of Consulting Psychology,* **30**: 381–387, 1966.

Crowne, D. P., and Marlowe, D. A new scale of social desirability independent of psychopathology. *Journal of Consulting Psychology,* **24**: 349–354, 1960.

Crumbaugh, J. C., Salzberg, H. C., and Agee, F. L. The effects of pool therapy on aggression. *Journal of Clinical Psychology,* **22**: 235–237, 1966.

DeLeon, G., and Mandell, W. A comparison of conditioning and psychotherapy in the treatment of functional enuresis. *Journal of Clinical Psychology,* **22**: 326–330, 1966.

Deutsch, F., and Murphy, W. F. *The Clinical Interview, Vol. 2: Therapy.* New York: International Universities Press, 1960.

DiMascio, A., and Brooks, G. W. Free association to a fantasied psychotherapist: a case report. *Archives of General Psychiatry,* **4**: 513–516, 1961.

Dohrenwend, Barbara S., and Dohrenwend, B. P. Field studies of social factors in relation to three types of psychological disorder. *Journal of Abnormal Psychology,* **72**: 369–378, 1967.

Dollard, J., and Miller, N. E. *Personality and Psychotherapy Change.* New York: McGraw-Hill, 1950.

Dreikurs, R. Technique and dynamics of multiple psychotherapy. *Psychiatric Quarterly,* **24**: 788–799, 1950.

Dublin, J. E., Elton, C. F., and Berzins, J. I. Some personality and aptitudinal correlates of the "A-B" therapist scale. *Journal of Consulting and Clinical Psychology,* **33**: 739–745, 1969.

Dunlap, K. *Habits: Their Making and Unmaking.* New York: Liveright, 1932.

Durant, W. *The Story of Civilization. Vol. IV. The Age of Faith.* New York: Simon and Schuster, 1950.

Eisenberg, L. The strategic deployment of the child psychiatrist in preventive psychiatry. *Journal of Child Psychology and Psychiatry,* **2**: 229–241, 1961.

English, H. B., and English, Ava C. *A Comprehensive Dictionary of Psychological and Psychoanalytical Terms.* New York: Longmans, Green, 1958.

English, O. S., and Finch, S. M. *Introduction to Psychiatry.* New York: Norton, 1954.

Erikson, E. Psychoanalysis and other therapies. *Psychiatry and Social Science Review,* **1** (May): 14–19, 1967.

Eysenck, H. J. The effects of psychotherapy. In H. J. Eysenck, ed. *Handbook of Abnormal Psychology.* New York: Basic Books, 1961.

Eysenck, H. J., and Rachman, S. *The Causes and Cures of Neurosis.* London: Routledge and Kegan Paul, 1965.

Federn, E. The therapeutic personality, as illustrated by Paul Federn and August Aichhorn. *Psychiatric Quarterly, 36*: 29–43, 1962.

Feifel, H., and Eells, J. Patients and therapists assess the same psychotherapy. *Journal of Consulting Psychology, 27*: 310–318, 1963.

Fenichel, O. *The Psychoanalytic Theory of Neurosis.* New York: Norton, 1945.

Fiedler, F. A. The concept of the ideal therapeutic relationship. *Journal of Consulting Psychology, 14*: 239–245, 1950a.

Fiedler, F. A. A comparison of therapeutic relationships in psychoanalytic, nondirective, and Adlerian therapy. *Journal of Consulting Psychology, 14*: 436–445, 1950b.

Finney, B. C., and Crockett, Norma D. Partnership therapy: A new technique. *Psychotherapy: Theory, Research and Practice, 2*: 136–138, 1965.

Fisher, K. S. The uses of perversity. *Psychotherapy: Theory, Research and Practice, 2*: 35–37, 1965.

Ford, D. H., and Urban, H. B. *Systems of Psychotherapy.* New York: Wiley, 1963.

Frank, G. H., and Sweetland, A. A study of the process of psychotherapy: the verbal interaction. *Journal of Consulting Psychology, 26*: 135–138, 1962.

Frank, J. D. *Persuasion and Healing.* Baltimore: Johns Hopkins Press, 1961.

Frankl, V. E. Paradoxical intention: a logotherapeutic technique. *American Journal of Psychotherapy, 14*: 520–525, 1960.

Freud, S. Analysis of a phobia in a five-year-old boy. In Strachey, J., ed. *Collected Papers.* Vol. 3. New York: Basic Books, 1959.

Freud, S. Two encyclopedia articles. In Strachey, J., ed. *Collected Papers.* Vol. 5. New York: Basic Books, 1959.

Friedman, H. J. Patient-expectancy and symptom reduction. *Archives of General Psychiatry, 8*: 61–67, 1963.

Garfield, S. L., and Kurz, M. Evaluation of treatment and related procedure in 1,216 cases referred to a mental hygiene clinic. *Psychiatric Quarterly, 26*: 414–424, 1952.

Geertsma, R. H., and Reivich, R. S. Repetitive self-observation by videotape playback. *Journal of Nervous and Mental Disease, 141*: 29–41, 1965.

Gerz, H. O. Experience with the logotherapeutic technique of paradoxical intention in treatment of phobic and obsessive-compulsive patients. *American Journal of Psychiatry, 123*: 548–553, 1966.

Ginott, H. G., Bleck, Libby, and Barnes, Ruby I. A study in nonattendance of initial interviews in a community clinic. *International Journal of Group Psychotherapy, 9*: 314–321, 1959.

Gittelman, M. Behavior rehearsal as a technique in child treatment. *Journal of Child Psychology and Psychiatry, 6*: 251–255, 1965.

Grotjahn, M., and Gabe, S. Psychotherapy—outline of its history and present situation. In Mikesell, E. H., ed. *Modern Abnormal Psychology.* New York: Philosophical Library, 1950.

Grünbaum, A. Causality and the science of human behavior. In Feigl, H., and Brodbeck, May, eds. *Readings in the Philosophy of Science.* New York: Appleton-Century-Crofts, 1953.

Guerney, B., Jr. Filial therapy: description and rationale. *Journal of Consulting Psychology,* **28**: 304–310, 1964.

Gundlach, R. H. Overview of outcome studies in group psychotherapy. *International Journal of Group Psychotherapy,* **17**: 196–210, 1967.

Hanson, J. C., Moore, G. D., and Carkhuff, R. R. The differential relationship of objective and client perceptions of counseling. *Journal of Clinical Psychology,* **24**: 244–246, 1968.

Hartmann, W. The free will controversy. *American Psychologist,* **16**: 37–38, 1961.

Hausner, M., and Dolezal, V. Follow-up studies in group and individual LSD psychotherapy. *Activitas Nervosa Superior,* **8**: 87–95, 1966.

Heath, R. G. Pleasure response of human subjects to direct stimulation of the brain: physiologic and psychodynamic considerations. In Heath, R. G., ed. *The Role of Pleasure in Behavior—a Symposium of 22 Authors.* New York: Harper and Row, 1964.

Heckel, R. V., Wiggins, S. L., and Salzberg, H. C. Conditioning against silences in group therapy. *Journal of Clinical Psychology,* **18**: 216–217, 1962.

Hein, G. W. A. Psychotherapeutic possibilities to overcome resistance to therapy with special attention to the psychoanalytic method. *Zeitschrift für Psychotherapie und medizinische Psychologie,* **13**: 81–87, 1963.

Heinicke, C. M., et al. Frequency of psychotherapeutic session as a factor affecting the child's developmental status. *Psychoanalytic Study of the Child,* **20**: 42–98, 1965.

Hersch, P. D., and Scheibe, K. E. Reliability and validity of internal-external control as a personality dimension. *Journal of Consulting Psychology,* **31**: 609–613, 1967.

Hinsie, L. E., and Shatsky, J. *Psychiatric Dictionary.* New York: Oxford, 1947.

Hobbs, N. Helping disturbed children: psychological and ecological strategies. *American Psychologist,* **21**: 1105–1115, 1966.

Hogan, R. A., and Kirchner, J. H. Preliminary report of the extinction of learned fears via short-term implosive therapy. *Journal of Abnormal Psychology,* **72**: 106–109, 1967.

Hovland, C. I. Effects of the mass media of communication. In Lindzey, G., ed. *Handbook of Social Psychology,* Vol. 2. Cambridge, Mass.: Addison-Wesley, 1954.

Imber, S. D., et al. Suggestibility, social class and the acceptance of psychotherapy. *Journal of Clinical Psychology,* **12**: 341–344, 1956.

Imber, S. D., et al. A ten year follow-up study of treated psychiatric outpatients. In Leese, S., ed. *An Evaluation of the Results of the Psychotherapies.* Springfield, Ill.: Thomas, 1968.

Imber, S. D., Frank, J. D., Nash, E. H., Stone, A. R., and Gleidman, L. H. Improvement and amount of therapeutic contact: an alternative to the use of no-treatment controls in psychotherapy. *Journal of Consulting Psychology,* **21**: 309–315, 1957.

Immergluck, L. Determinism—freedom in contemporary psychology: an ancient problem revisited. *American Psychologist,* **19**: 270–281, 1964.

Johnson, D. L., et al. Human relations training for psychiatric patients: a follow-up study. *International Journal of Social Psychiatry,* **11**: 188–196, 1965.

Jones, E. *The Life and Work of Sigmund Freud.* Vol. 2. New York: Basic Books, 1955.

Jones, Mary C. A laboratory study of fear: the case of Peter. *Pedagogical Seminary,* **31**: 308–315, 1924.

Jones, N. F., and Kahn, M. W. Patient attitudes as related to social class and other variables concerned with hospitalization. *Journal of Consulting Psychology,* **28**: 403–408, 1964.

Kasman, Joyce V., Griffin, W. V., and Mauritzen, J. H. Effect of environmental surroundings on outpatients' mood and perception of psychiatrists. *Journal of Consulting and Clinical Psychology,* **32**: 223–226, 1968.

Kawabata, T. Reupbringing psychotherapy. *Japanese Journal of Child Psychiatry,* **6**: 228–240, 1966.

Kidd, A. H., and Walton, Nancy Y. Dart throwing as a method of reducing extra-punitive aggression. *Psychological Reports,* **19**: 88–90, 1966.

Kiesler, D. J. Some myths of psychotherapy research and the search for a paradigm. *Psychological Bulletin,* **65**: 110–136, 1966.

Klein, W., and Zax, M. The use of a hospital volunteer program in the teaching of abnormal psychology. *Journal of Social Psychology,* **65**: 155–165, 1965.

Kluge, — and, Thren, — . Beldstreifendenken als psychotherapeutische Methode (Mental motion pictures as a psychotherapeutic method). *Zeitschrift für Psychotherapie und medizinische Psychologie,* **1**: 13–20, 1951.

Knight, G. Stereotactic trachotomy in the surgical treatment of mental illness. *Journal of Neurology, Neurosurgery and Psychiatry,* **28**: 304–310, 1965.

Kora, T., and Sato, K. Morita therapy: a psychotherapy in the way of Zen. *Psychologia,* **1**: 219–225, 1958.

Krasner, L. The therapist as a social reinforcement machine. In Strupp, H. H., and Luborsky, L., eds. *Research in Psychotherapy.* Washington, D. C.: American Psychological Association, 1962.

Krasner, L. Reinforcement, verbal behavior, and psychotherapy. *American Journal of Orthopsychiatry,* **33**: 601–613, 1963.

Lafall, J. The therapeutic attitude in treatment and management of chronic patients. *Psychotherapy: Theory, Research and Practice,* **2**: 28–30, 1965.

Laurence, S. B. Video tape and other therapeutic procedures with nude marathon groups. *American Psychologist,* **24**: 476–479, 1969.

Lazarus, A. A. Behavior rehearsal vs. non-directive therapy vs. advice in effecting behavior change. *Behavior Research and Therapy,* **4**: 209–212, 1966.

Lefcourt, H. M. Internal versus external control of reinforcement: a review. *Psychological Bulletin,* **65**: 206–220, 1966.

Levine, M. *Psychotherapy in Medical Practice.* New York: Macmillan, 1948.

Levinson, B. M. Pet psychotherapy: use of household pets in the treatment of behavior disorder in childhood. *Psychological Reports,* **17**: 695–698, 1965.

Levis, D. J., and Carrera, R. Effects of ten hours of implosive therapy in the treatment of outpatients: a preliminary report. *Journal of Abnormal Psychology,* **77**: 504–508, 1967.

Life Editors. *The Life Treasury of American Folklore.* New York: Time, Inc., 1961.

Linden, J. I., and Stollak, G. E. The training of undergraduates in play technique. *Journal of Clinical Psychology,* **25**: 213–218, 1969.

Lorr, M. Client perceptions of therapists: a study of the therapeutic relation. *Journal of Consulting Psychology,* **29**: 146–149, 1965.

Lorr, M., McNair, D. M., Michaux, W. W., and Riskin, A. Frequency of treatment and change in psychotherapy. *Journal of Abnormal and Social Psychology,* **64**: 281–292, 1962.

Mabbott, J. D. Free will. *Encyclopaedia Britannica,* Vol. 9, 855–859, 1967.

Mariner, A. S. A critical look at professional education in the mental health field. *American Psychologist,* **22**: 271–281, 1967.

Marlowe, D. Need for social approval and the operant conditioning of meaningful verbal behavior. *Journal of Consulting Psychology,* **26**: 79–83, 1962.

Maslow, A. W., and Mittelman, B. *Principles of Abnormal Psychology.* New York: Harper, 1951.

Masserman, J. H. Faith and delusion in psychotherapy. *American Journal of Psychiatry,* **110**: 324–333, 1953.

May, R. The existential approach. In Arieti, S., ed. *American Handbook of Psychiatry.* Vol. 2. New York: Basic Books, 1959.

May, R. *Love and Will.* New York: W. W. Norton, 1969.

May, R., Angel, E., and Ellenberger, H. F., eds. *Existence: a New Dimension in Psychiatry and Psychology.* New York: Basic Books, 1958.

McMahon, J. T. The working class psychiatric patient: a clinical view. In Riessman, F., Cohen, J., and Peal, A., eds. *Mental Health of the Poor.* New York: Free Press of Glencoe, 1964.

McNair, D. M., Callahan, D. M., and Lorr, M. Therapist "type" and patient response to psychotherapy. *Journal of Consulting Psychology,* **26**: 425–429, 1962.

Medina, G. S. Psychotrial: a new type of group therapy. *Corrective Psychiatry and Journal of Social Therapy,* **11**: 157–162, 1965.

Mendelsohn, G. A., and Rankin, N. O. Client-counselor compatibility and the outcome of counseling. *Journal of Abnormal Psychology,* **74**: 157–163, 1969.

Menninger, K. *Theory of Psychoanalytic Technique.* New York: Basic Books, 1958.

Mensh, I. N., and Golden, Janet M. Factors in psychotherapeutic success. *Journal of Missouri Medical Association,* **48**: 180–184, 1951.

Michaux, W. W., and Lorr, M. Psychotherapists' treatment goals. *Journal of Counseling Psychology,* **8**: 250–254, 1961.

Miller, Ira. On taking notes. *International Journal of Psychoanalysis,* **46**: 121–122, 1964.

Mora, G. Recent American psychiatric developments. In Arieti, S., ed. *American Handbook of Psychiatry.* Vol. 1. New York: Basic Books, 1959.

Moreno, Zerka T. A survey of psychodramatic techniques. *Group Psychotherapy,* **12**: 5–14, 1959.

Morgan, C. T. *Introduction to Psychology.* New York: McGraw-Hill, 1961.

Morgan, R. W. Is it scientific to be optimistic? *Social Work,* **6**: 12–21, 1961.

Moss, C. S. Visitation to mental health programs in Eastern Europe. *American Psychologist,* **22**: 452–456, 1967.

Mowrer, O. H., and Mowrer, W. M. Enuresis: a method for its study and treatment. *American Journal of Orthopsychiatry,* **8**: 436–459, 1938.

Muehlberg, Nancy, Pierce, R., and Drasgow, J. A factor analysis of therapeutically facilitative conditions. *Journal of Clinical Psychology,* **25**: 93–95, 1969.

Muench, G. A. An investigation of the efficacy of time-limited psychotherapy. *Journal of Counseling Psychology,* **12**: 294–298, 1965.

Nahemow, Lucille. Comparison of users and nonusers at a community mental health facility. Paper presented at American Psychological Association Convention, 1968.

Nash, E. H., et al. Some factors related to patients remaining in group psychotherapy. *International Journal of Group Psychotherapy,* **7**: 264–274, 1957.

Nash, E. H., Frank, J. D., Gliedman, L. H., Imber, S. D., and Stone, A. R. Some factors related to patients remaining in group psychotherapy. *International Journal of Group Psychotherapy,* **7**: 264–274, 1957.

Nash, M. M., and Zimring, F. M. Prediction of reaction to placebo. *Journal of Abnormal Psychology,* **74**: 568–573, 1969.

Neilson, W. A., ed. *Webster's New International Dictionary of the English Language.* Springfield, Mass.: Merriam, 1952.

N.I.M.H. *Psychologists in Mental Health.* USPHS Publication 1557, 1966.

Norton, J. Treatment of a dying patient. In Eisler, R., et al., eds. *The Psychoanalytic Study of the Child.* Vol. 18. New York: International Universities Press, 1963.

Noyes, A. P. *Modern Clinical Psychiatry.* Philadelphia: W. B. Saunders, 1948.

Orlinsky, D. E., and Howard, K. I. The good therapy hour: experiential correlates of patients' and therapists' evaluations of therapy sessions. *Archives of General Psychiatry,* **16**: 621–632, 1967.

Paige, A. B., McNamara, H. J., and Fisch, R. I. A preliminary report on sensory stimulative therapy with chronic schizophrenic patients. *Psychotherapy: Theory, Research and Practice,* **1**: 133–136, 1964.

Parker, G. V. C. Some concomitants of therapist dominance in the psychotherapy interview. *Journal of Consulting Psychology,* **31**: 313–318, 1967.

Patterson, C. H. *Theories of Counseling and Psychotherapy.* New York: Harper and Row, 1966.

Pattison, E. M. Evaluation studies of group psychotherapy. *International Journal of Group Psychotherapy,* **15**: 382–397, 1965.

Paul, G. L. Strategy of outcome research in psychotherapy. *Journal of Consulting Psychology,* 109–118, 1967.

Pfeiffer, E. Patients as therapists. *American Journal of Psychiatry,* **123**: 1413–1418, 1967.

Pines, Maya. Training housewives as psychotherapists. *Harper's,* **224**: 37–42, 1962.

Polatin, P., and Philtine, Ellen C. *How Psychiatry Helps.* New York: Harper, 1949.

Poser, E. G. The effect of therapists' training on group therapeutic outcomes. *Journal of Consulting Psychology,* **30**: 283–289, 1966.

Powdermaker, F. B., and Frank, J. D. *Group Psychotherapy.* Cambridge: Harvard University Press, 1953.

Rank, O. *Art and Artist.* New York: Alfred Knopf, 1932.

Regardie, F. I. Active psychotherapy. *Complex,* **7**: 3–14, 1952.

Reisman, J. M. *The Development of Clinical Psychology.* New York: Appleton-Century-Crofts, 1966.

Reisman, J. M. Ratings of self and therapist: two studies. *Psychiatric Quarterly Supplement,* **42**: 116–123, 1968.

Riesman, D., Glazer, N., and Denney, R. *The Lonely Crowd.* Garden City, N. Y.: Doubleday Anchor, 1955.

Riese, Hertha, *Heal the Hurt Child.* Chicago: University of Chicago Press, 1962.

Robertiello, R. C., Friedman, D. B., and Pollens, B. *The Analyst's Role.* New York: Citadel, 1963.

Rogers, C. R. *Counseling and Psychotherapy.* New York: Houghton Mifflin, 1942.

Rogers, C. R. *Client-Centered Therapy.* Boston: Houghton Mifflin, 1951.

Rogers, C. R. The necessary and sufficient conditions of therapeutic personality change. *Journal of Consulting Psychology,* **21**: 95–103, 1957.

Rogers, C. R. *On Becoming a Person.* Boston: Houghton Mifflin, 1961.

Rogers, C. R. Some learnings from a study of psychotherapy with schizophrenics. *Pennsylvania Psychiatric Quarterly,* 3–15, 1962.

Rogers, C. R. The therapeutic relationship: recent theory and research. *Australian Journal of Psychology,* **17**: 95–108, 1965.

Rogers, C. R., ed. *The Therapeutic Relationship and Its Impact: a Study of Psychotherapy with Schizophrenics.* Madison: University of Wisconsin Press, 1967.

Rogers, C. R., and Dymond, Rosalind F., eds. *Psychotherapy and Personality Change.* Chicago: University of Chicago Press, 1954.

Romano, J. Psychotherapy. In Witmer, Helen L., ed. *Teaching Psychotherapeutic Medicine.* New York: Commonwealth Fund, 1947.

Rosanoff, A. J. *Manual of Psychiatry.* New York: Wiley, 1947.

Rosen, J. N. *Direct Analysis.* New York: Grune & Stratton, 1953.

Rosenthal, R. *Experimenter Effects in Behavioral Research.* New York: Appleton-Century-Crofts, 1966.

Rotter, J. B. Generalized expectancies for internal versus external control of reinforcement. *Psychological Monographs,* **80** (1), Whole No. 609, 1966.

Rotter, J. B., Liverant, S., and Crowne, D. P. The growth and extinction of expectancies in chance controlled and skilled tasks. *Journal of Psychology,* **52**: 161–177, 1961.

Ruesch, J. *Therapeutic Communication.* New York: Norton, 1961.

Sager, C. J. Freedom and psychotherapy. *American Journal of Psychotherapy,* **13**: 4–17, 1959.

Sarason, S. B. *Psychological Problems in Mental Deficiency.* New York: Harper & Row, 1949.

Saul, L. J. A note on the telephone as a technical aid. *Psychoanalytic Quarterly,* **20**: 287–290, 1951.

Saul, L. J. On the value of one or two interviews. *Psychoanalytic Quarterly,* **20**: 613–615, 1951.

Scher, J. M., II. Primary gain: the game of illness and the communicative compact in the borderline patient. *Psychiatric Quarterly,* **35**: 523–543, 1961.

Schroeder, Pearl. Client acceptance of responsibility and difficulty of psychotherapy. *Journal of Consulting Psychology,* **24**: 467, 471, 1960.

Schwitzgebel, R. L. Therapeutic research: a procedure for the reduction of adolescent crime. Paper presented at American Psychological Association Convention, 1963.

Schwitzgebel, R. L. A belt from Big Brother. *Psychology Today,* 45–47, 65, April 1969.

Sears, R. R., Whiting, J. W. M., Nowlis, V., and Sears, Pauline S. Some child-rearing antecedents of aggression and dependency in young children. *Genetic Psychology Monographs,* **47**: 135–234, 1953.

Sears, R. R., Maccoby, E., and Levin, H. *Patterns of Child Rearing.* Evanston, Ill.: Tow, Peterson, 1957.

Shapiro, S. B. *Six Modern Therapies: Instructor's Manual.* Chicago: Scott, Foresman, 1964.

Sheperd, M., Oppenheim, A. N., and Mitchell, S. Childhood behavior disorders and the child guidance clinic. *Journal of Child Psychology and Psychiatry,* **7**: 39–52, 1966.

Sherman, M. H. Siding with the resistance in paradigmatic therapy. *Psychoanalytic Review,* **48**: 43–45, 1961.

Shlien, J. M., Mosak, H. H., and Dreikurs, R. Effect of time limits: a comparison of two psychotherapies. *Journal of Counseling Psychology,* **9**: 31–34, 1962.

Shoben, E. J. Some observations on psychotherapy and the learning process. In Mowrer, O. H., ed. *Psychotherapy Theory and Research.* New York: Ronald, 1953.

Shostrom, E. L., and Riley, Clara M. D. Parametric analysis of psychotherapy. *Journal of Consulting and Clinical Psychology,* **32**: 628–632, 1968.

Slavson, S. R. *A Textbook in Analytic Group Psychotherapy*. New York: International Universities Press, 1964.

Smith, A. B., Bassin, A., and Froehlich, A. Change in attitudes and degree of verbal participation in group therapy with adult offenders. *Journal of Consulting Psychology*, **24**: 247–249, 1960.

Speisman, J. C. Depth of interpretation and verbal resistance in psychotherapy. *Journal of Consulting Psychology*, **23**: 93–99, 1959.

Stampfl, T. G., and Levis, D. J. Essentials of implosive therapy: a learning-theory-based psychodynamic behavioral therapy. *Journal of Abnormal Psychology*, **77**: 496–503, 1967.

Steinzer, B. *The Healing Partnership: The Patient as Colleague in Psychotherapy*. New York: Harper & Row, 1967.

Stevenson, I. Process of "spontaneous" recovery from the psychoneuroses. *American Journal of Psychiatry*, **117**: 1057–1064, 1961.

Stieper, D. R., and Wiener, D. N. The problem of interminability in outpatient psychotherapy. *Journal of Consulting Psychology*, **23**: 237–242, 1959.

Stieper, D. R., and Wiener, D. N. *Dimensions of Psychotherapy*. Chicago: Aldine, 1965.

Strupp, H. H. The performance of psychoanalytic and client-centered therapists in an initial interview. *Journal of Consulting Psychology*, **22**: 265–274, 1958.

Sullivan, H. S. *The Psychiatric Interview*. New York: Norton, 1954.

Sundland, D. M., and Barker, E. N. The orientations of psychotherapists. *Journal of Consulting Psychology*, **26**: 201–212, 1962.

Taft, Jessie. *Dynamics of Therapy*. New York: Macmillan, 1933.

Thorp, R. G. Psychological patterning in marriage. *Psychological Bulletin*, **60**: 97–117, 1963.

Tiffany, D. W. Mental health: a function of experienced control. *Journal of Clinical Psychology*, **23**: 311–315, 1967.

Time, 72, July 28, 1967.

Titchener, E. B. *An Outline of Psychology*. New York: Macmillan, 1902.

Tolor, A. Teachers' evaluations of children in short-term treatment with subprofessionals. *Journal of Clinical Psychology*, **24**: 377–378, 1968.

Tolstoy, L. Some words about "War and Peace." In *War and Peace*, Vol. 2. New York: Heritage Press, 1938.

Towbin, A. P. Self-care unit. *Journal of Consulting and Clinical Psychology*, **33**: 561–570, 1969.

Truax, C. B. Reinforcement and nonreinforcement in Rogerian psychotherapy. *Journal of Abnormal Psychology*, **71**: 1–9, 1966.

Truax, C. B., and Carkhuff, R. R. For better or for worse: the process of psychotherapeutic change. In *Recent Advances in Behavioral Change*. Montreal: McGill University Press, 1964.

Truax, C. B., and Carkhuff, R. R. *Toward Effective Counseling and Psychotherapy: Training and Practice*. Chicago: Aldine, 1967.

Truax, C. B., Wargo, D. G., and Silber, L. D. Effects of group psychotherapy with high accurate empathy and nonpossessive warmth upon female institutionalized delinquents. *Journal of Abnormal Psychology,* **71**: 267–274, 1966.

Truax, C. B., et al. Therapist empathy, genuineness, and warmth and patient therapeutic outcome. *Journal of Consulting Psychology,* **30**: 395–401, 1966.

Truax, C. B., Fine, H., Moravec, J., and Millis, W. Effects of therapist persuasive potency in individual psychotherapy. *Journal of Clinical Psychology,* **24**: 359–362, 1968.

Turner, R. H. Dithering devices in the classroom: how to succeed in shaking up a campus without really trying. *American Psychologist,* **21**: 957–963, 1966.

Turner, R. H., and Vanderlippe, R. H. Self-ideal congruence as an index of adjustment. *Journal of Abnormal and Social Psychology,* **57**: 202–206, 1958.

Ulmann, L. P., and Krasner, L. *A Psychological Approach to Abnormal Behavior.* Englewood Cliffs, N. J.: Prentice-Hall, 1969.

University of the State of New York. *Handbook 51: Psychology.* Albany: State Education Department, 1961.

Vesprani, G. J. Personality correlates of accurate empathy in a college companion program. *Journal of Consulting and Clinical Psychology,* **33**: 722–727, 1969.

Waldfogel, S., and Gardner, G. E. Intervention in crises as a method of primary prevention: In Caplan, G., ed. *Prevention of Mental Disorders in Children.* New York: Basic Books, 1961.

Weisman, M. N., Mann, Lenora, and Barker, B. W. Camping: an approach to releasing human potential in chronic mental patients. *American Journal of Psychiatry,* **123**: 166–172, 1966.

Whitaker, Dorothy S., and Lieberman, M. A. *Psychotherapy through the Group Process.* New York: Atherton, 1964.

White, R. W. *The Abnormal Personality.* New York: Ronald, 1964.

Whitehorn, J. C. Psychotherapy. In Harris, N. G., ed. *Modern Trends in Psychological Medicine.* New York: Hoeber, 1948.

Whitehorn, J. C., and Betz, Barbara J. A study of psychotherapeutic relationship between physicians and schizophrenic patients. *American Journal of Psychiatry,* **111**: 321–331, 1954.

Widroe, H., and Davidson, Joan. The use of directed writing in psychotherapy. *Bulletin of the Menninger Clinic,* **25**: 110–119, 1961.

Winder, C. L. Psychotherapy. *Annual Review of Psychology,* **8**: 309–330, 1957.

Winder, C. L., Ahmad, F. Z., Bandura, A., and Row, L. C. Dependency of patients, psychotherapist's responses, and aspects of psychotherapy. *Journal of Consulting Psychology,* **26**: 129–134, 1962.

Wittson, Cecil L., Affleck, D. C., and Johnson, V. Two-way television in group therapy. *Mental Hospital,* **12**: 22–23, 1961.

Wolberg, L. R. *The Technique of Psychotherapy.* 2nd edition. Part 1. New York: Grune and Stratton, 1967.

Wolberg, L. R. *Short-Term Psychotherapy*. New York: Grune and Stratton, 1965.

Wolfensberger, W. The free will controversy. *American Psychologist,* **16**: 36–37, 1961.

Wolpe, J. *Psychotherapy by Reciprocal Inhibition*. Stanford: Stanford University Press, 1958.

Wolpe, J. Psychotherapy: the nonscientific heritage and the new science. *Behavior Research and Therapy,* **1**: 23–28, 1963.

Wolpe, J., and Lazarus, A. A. *Behavior Therapy Techniques: A Guide to the Treatment of Neuroses*. Oxford: Pergamon Press, 1966.

Yates, D. H. Psychotherapy. In Harriman, P. L., ed. *Encyclopedia of Psychology*. New York: Citadel, 1951.

Yulia, S., and Kiesler, D. J. Countertransference response as a function of therapist anxiety and content of patient talk. *Journal of Consulting and Clinical Psychology,* **32**: 413–419, 1968.

Ziferstein, I. The Soviet psychiatrist: his relationship to his patients and to his society. *American Journal of Psychiatry,* **123**: 440–446, 1966.

Index